Modern American History

A Captivating Guide to the Modern History of the United States of America

Free Bonus from Captivating History
(Available for a Limited time)

Hi History Lovers!

Now you have a chance to join our exclusive history list so you can get your first history ebook for free as well as discounts and a potential to get more history books for free! Simply visit the link below to join.

Captivatinghistory.com/ebook

Also, make sure to follow us on Facebook, Twitter and Youtube by searching for Captivating History.

Contents

Introduction

We will start this book with the 1920s, a time often seen as being filled with glitz and glamor. Several decades before, the Civil War had ended, which made the North/South divide even clearer. It left generations of Black Americans trying to recuperate from the effects of slavery.

By the 1920s, WWI had also taken its toll on the United States, leaving citizens wondering why they took part in the first place. It gave them an isolationist outlook on the world, yet people still wanted to live their lives in a free fashion. This is similar to how global communities feel after living through the COVID-19 pandemic.

The 1920s was a pinnacle time in the United States in many ways. For instance, it was a time when women were breaking free from the typical social construct of what was previously expected from them. It was when the social experiment of Prohibition began. For those unfamiliar with the term, US society was banned from consuming and selling alcohol. This brought up important questions, such as if it should be possible for a government to ban certain types of liquids for the "good" of society?

We will also be looking at what war truly is. After all, the 20th century saw many types of wars, the Second World War being one of them. Like the world war before it, World War Two brought significant changes to society. This book examines these changes and how they changed not only the United States but also society globally. The global community was certainly impacted by this war, as well as the following war: the Cold War. Each move the United States and its rival, the Soviet Union, made affected continents around the world, even though the two nations never directly fought each other.

What exactly was the Cold War, though? And can a war actually be "cold" when nations are involved in proxy wars due to the tensions between capitalist and communist societies? That's a question for consideration when reading about the events of the 20th century.

This book will also delve into wars where it's not clear who the enemy is, in particular when discussing the war in Vietnam and the famous "War on Terror." We will talk about things that Americans and citizens around the world are struggling with even today. For instance, we will uncover what makes a person a terrorist and the different types of terrorism, both domestic (in regards to the United States) and international.

The economy has often been mentioned in recent US news, and that was no different in the past. We will cover what Americans thought about when it came to how much the government should interfere in the economy. The development of this process will be discussed by looking at the dips and rises that happened during the 20th century and how the presidents of the time ignored or jumped into solving the problems.

And, of course, a book on modern American history would be incomplete without looking at the movements of the mid-1900s. We will look at how everyday Americans found their voice fighting for their rights in the 1950s and the decade after, which resulted in the peak of protests during the late 1960s. Furthermore, we will cover different groups of people, such as Black Americans, women, the poor, and the LGBTQ community.

The events involving America are multi-layered. Many people have their own opinions on the decisions politicians and world leaders made at that time. Looking back, it's clear to see why certain decisions were made, but the complexity of each event may never be fully revealed.

Chapter 1 – The Roaring Twenties

What Was the Roaring Twenties?

The 1920s in the United States had many layers. It was a time when industry was booming, and new jobs were created. It was also a time when alcohol was banned, which led to a shift in American society. This ban showed the people how important alcohol had become in Western society. The decade brought forth many new things, including modern products, dances, and fashion choices, some of which are present in today's society.

The 1920s saw the continually changing role women had in society and at home. The Americans had suffered the consequences of fighting in World War One, as well as the devastation of the Spanish Flu. Thus, during these years, they were in a state of recovery, but the future seemed promising. However, the people were surprised to find this wasn't the case. Even though the decade was flamboyant and notorious, it was the prelude to the Great Depression.

The glamor and the hardships of the 1920s make it interesting to delve into. One's view of the 1920s could be seen as entirely positive or riddled with negativity. This chapter will look at both sides of the coin, giving you the chance to decide for yourself.

Prohibition

The 1920s have been portrayed as a time of high living. It was not labeled the "Roaring Twenties" for nothing. One of the reasons the time was like no other is because of the "P" word: Prohibition. Prohibition officially began at the start of the 1920s. The Volstead Act, also known as the National Prohibition Act, had been passed the previous year. This act enforced the Eighteenth Amendment, which had been ratified in 1919 and came into effect in mid-January 1920. The Volstead Act banned the selling of alcohol, and it also made it illegal to transport or produce alcohol.

The Prohibition movement started approximately a century before the Volstead Act came to pass. Groups formed to make a change in their community. Plenty of people had seen the way that alcohol changed people. For example, some husbands would get paid after a long week of working hard and spend their earnings straightaway in a local drinking establishment. This sometimes resulted in them returning home drunk and, in serious cases, beating their wives. Movements, such as the temperance movement, which began in the early 1800s, although it began to pick up steam in the 1820s, wanted to fight against what they saw as alcohol tearing households apart. Their fight for Prohibition stopped during the Civil War but gained momentum again afterward.

The fight against alcohol continued into the 1880s. Due to the work of the temperance movement, the Prohibition Party (the third-longest active party in the US today) and the Woman's Christian Temperance Union, towns began to make it illegal to sell alcohol. Some towns even took it a step further and made it illegal to drink alcohol as well.

A year into the 1880s, Prohibition on a national level began to build momentum. For instance, selling and drinking alcohol was made illegal in all of Kansas. January 17th, 1920, was a date that many Americans would have remembered during this decade: it was the day that selling alcohol was officially banned nationwide. It is important to remember that although alcohol was banned, there were still numerous groups of people who did not approve of the new law. They would find ways to put hard spirits into the hands of hardworking Americans.

Prohibition and Its Effects

There were many effects of Prohibition. The first one is quite understandable. What would you do if you loved coffee and heard that you would no longer be able to purchase it? I assume the answer is that you would either begin to produce it yourself or buy a lot of it, ensuring you had a long-lasting supply. Well, that's exactly what happened during Prohibition.

Although a lot of alcohol from breweries was destroyed, members of the public stockpiled much of the existing alcohol. A huge fraction of the public still wanted to consume alcohol, and people began to make wine at home. A loophole in the law allowed households to produce wine as long as it was not going to be sold. The law stated households could not produce more than two hundred gallons per year.

Another part of Prohibition that is often glamorized is the speakeasies. Many films portray these as a relaxed and popular way to have a casual drink in the 1920s, and these films are not wrong. Speakeasies were underground drinking establishments that would often have live music. They took place in unsuspecting locations like cafes and basements. If you purchased alcohol in a speakeasy, you would be purchasing alcohol illegally. People from all walks of life went to them. On any given day, you could have found a judge, police officer, or hairdresser at a speakeasy. You would have also found members of both the Democrat and Republican Parties at a speakeasy. Speakeasies often had special passwords that people used to gain entry. This was to ensure that the police, at least those who would bust the owners and patrons, would not be able to gain access.

Banning alcohol was encouraged because it was preached as a way to better society. It even seemed like alcoholism went down during the beginning of the 1920s. This argument was preached until the bitter end when Prohibition ended in 1933 and even afterward by certain groups.

Unfortunately, Prohibition wasn't all positive. People who worked in saloons, bars, and breweries before Prohibition lost their jobs. Additionally, the crime scene changed and not for the better. The previously mentioned speakeasies were usually run by criminals. Prohibition enabled the rise of well-known criminals like Al Capone and crime syndicates, which became rich by importing alcohol from countries where it was still legal to consume.

And that is not the end of it. The police officers who didn't agree with Prohibition were easy to pay off and even visited speakeasies. This meant some officers would have been involved with criminals, many of whom did more than just sell alcohol. This level of corruption even reached people in higher places, such as judges.

However, there were some people who did enforce the law. They were commonly known as Prohibition officers. These officers often made headline news for seizing countless amounts of alcohol. Headlines like "31 Arrested in DC Bootleg Raids" were common and often included pictures of officers looking proudly at the alcohol they had seized.[ii]

An image of Prohibition officers destroying barrels of alcohol
https://en.wikipedia.org/wiki/File:Prohibition_agents_destroying_barrels_of_alcohol_(United_States,_pro hibition_era).jpg.

The End of Prohibition

Prohibition lasted for thirteen years. During these thirteen years, many people decided the original intention of Prohibition had not worked. Society had changed, and in some ways, people blamed the rise in crime and corruption on the alcohol ban. Many began to call for change. It came to an end during Franklin Delano Roosevelt's time as president of the United States of America.

Technology

Electricity: Radios and New Products

One of the changes that make a huge impact on society is the development of technology. Inventors began to utilize electricity in a new way during the 1920s. Companies like General Electric were able to transport electrical power quicker than ever before. Technological advancements like these paved the way for more households to become wired. The beginning of the 1920s saw a third of the population have running electricity in their homes. This meant households had the opportunity to use electrical appliances more conveniently.

More households with electricity meant more appliances. Appliances like the washing machine and the vacuum cleaner became must-haves. They were marketed as necessary for a home in the 1920s due to the fact that they would save housewives time when doing chores around the house. It was also important for the modern woman who was trying to make her mark in the workforce during this era since it lessened the amount of time one had to spend on chores.

One of the most popular devices that were used in the 1920s was the radio. Owning a radio became popular in the 1920s, and it was soon a must-have for American households. Although the first American transatlantic broadcast signal happened in the early 1900s, the first commercial broadcast happened in 1920 from KDKA out of Pittsburgh.[iii] Many people did not have a radio then, but the broadcast was the start of things to come. The United States had over five hundred radio stations broadcasting by 1922, and sales for the device were heavily increasing. By the end of the decade, radio content ranged from advertisements to Sunday services. Soap operas and even shows for children were broadcast on the radio.

The way in which electricity was used in the 1920s changed society. It became possible for people to purchase appliances and inventions that were simply not widely available before. Due to the mass use of electricity in the 1920s, it is no wonder that 90 percent of American households had electricity in their homes by the start of the next decade. Advanced technology had become the norm. It was a time of reaping the fruits of the technological discoveries that had happened before the decade.

The Economy in the US

How Did Consumerism Lead to the Great Depression?

The development of technology brought about a new mindset within society. With every new appliance, such as the washing machine or the refrigerator, there was also an advertisement that told customers that they needed the product. Nowadays, we are bombarded with new devices that will make our lives better and easier, and the 1920s were no different. This was the birth of consumerism in America. To give consumers more buying power, US President Calvin Coolidge, who was president from 1923 to 1929, reduced the amount of taxes the population had to pay, which indeed gave consumers more money to spend.

Elements of the 1920s were glamourous; however, it was not all rosy. Many families had more income in this era. However, everyone was not in the same boat, and some families could not afford to live up to the standard that was set for them. Consumers began to buy products with credit, and some bought products in installments. This meant that, on the surface, many households looked affluent due to the objects they had bought. But when one delved into their finances, one would see that just because they had these items, they were not necessarily well-off. Even though this is true, since the economy was doing well, people had faith that it would stay that way. Except for some economists, most people did not see what was coming.

The same financial ideas were brought to the stock market. More individuals were able to invest in it, and at the end of the decade, millions of Americans had stocks and shares. Similar to purchasing products, both individuals and investors often bought stocks in installments, and some consumers bought stocks and shares with credit. This kind of financial thinking was what led the economy down the path of destruction in the late 1920s.

The economy in the 1920s looked healthy, though. There was a recession at the beginning of the decade, but after this, the economy moved in a positive direction. Technology had a part to play in this healthy economy. Due to Henry Ford's visionary idea of constructing an automobile by using an assembly line, many factories adopted the idea and were able to create products using Ford's method. This led to many products being mass-produced, which meant they could and were indeed sold at a lower price.

During this time, cars were being produced at an extraordinary rate, which created jobs in other industries, such as oil and steel. Roads that were of better quality needed to be constructed too. This allowed the economy to boom, with jobs being created to boost the expanding industries.

Culture

Jazz music boomed in the 1920s. It is thought to come from New Orleans, and the music birthed famous dances. Music lovers would often congregate in clubs to listen to musicians like Ella Fitzgerald, and they often congregated in speakeasies to enjoy the music of the decade. The mass migration of African Americans to the North also sparked off a new era of music and literature called the Harlem Renaissance. It made Harlem a vibrant place for music, fashion, theater, literature, and much more.

Although the Harlem Renaissance is often seen as producing uplifting art, it also produced political forms of art. Writers such as Langston Hughes wrote about gaining racial equality. They wrote about the experiences that Black people and Native Americans had. One can see this in Langston Hughes's famous line, "America never was America to me." This quote originated from his well-known poem "Let America Be America Again."[iv]

Women and Traditions

The view of women had been changing in the previous decades. At the end of the 1800s, women had begun to change their outfits and wore clothes that had less of a Victorian look. This change and many more continued to occur in the 1920s.

Many women decided to lay down the old traditions of the past and bring in a new era. The multitudes of images that we see of the 1920s include the flapper. Flappers would wear knee-length dresses without stockings, a necklace made out of beads, and lots of makeup.

Looking at this image now, it does not seem controversial. In many cultures around the world nowadays, wearing a knee-length skirt or dress is considered normal. It was not, however, in those days.

An image of Josephine Baker performing the Charleston, a famous dance in the 1920s
https://commons.wikimedia.org/wiki/File:Baker_Charleston.jpg

Flappers moved away from acting in a manner that was seen as ladylike at that time. They swore, they drove, and they were independent. WWI has been blamed for the arrival of this attitude and fashion trends the young generation had at the time.' Young people wanted freedom from the past and from the restraints of the generation before. As you can imagine, every social group had an opinion of flappers, and they did not all see flappers in a positive light. This was especially true for people who wanted the traditional way of life to continue to be a part of American culture.

Women and Politics

The story of the American woman in the 1920s is not straightforward. The place of a woman had been changing since their fight for the right to vote in the mid-1800s. This paused during the Civil War but picked up momentum afterward. Officially, women gained the right to vote nationally in 1920. However, when the law was passed, many African American women were prevented and discouraged from voting. Although this improved in the 1960s, voting suppression is an issue many people of color face even to this day in the United States.[vi]

Before women gained the right to vote, women's organizations put this as their main focus. When this was achieved, the organizations began to focus on the many areas that affected women. Black suffragists focused on fighting against Jim Crow laws and making lynching illegal, which officially became illegal over a century after the fight in 2022.[vii] Organizations like the National Women's Party (NWP) focused on the interests of middle-class women. The lack of unity could have been the reason many women found it hard to make the mark on politics that they were truly looking for. On the other hand, the various intentions of the women's organizations show us the level of inequality that women experienced in all walks of life.

Women in the Workforce

A women's place in the workforce in the 1920s has many layers. Women's roles in World War I have often been discussed. Since many of the men fought in the war, women took up the jobs they would have been doing. However, this movement did not last. After the war, the women who were working jobs that were normally done by men lost them when the men returned. Professions that were often seen as women-dominated arenas one hundred years later were the types of jobs that were respectable for women to do in the 1920s. These jobs included working as teachers and social workers.

There are so many events and factors that encompass the 1920s. The continual fight for equality for women is just one of them. The fight for equality neither started nor ended in the 1920s, but it certainly took great steps in progressing a woman's place in society. The social experiment of Prohibition is an example of what happens when society is banned from doing something they think is important, driving even the average Joe into breaking the law.

Looking at the consumeristic culture in the 1920s is like looking in the mirror today in 2022. The idea of needing must-have products took hold of the culture then, and it continues to do so now. The mass production of the automobile changed life greatly. The idea of being able to produce them quickly changed the industry and spread to other factory owners, which, in turn, helped them to mass-produce more products for individuals in the United States.

Chapter 2 – The Great Depression and the New Deal

The Real Start of the 1930s

To talk about the 1930s, we first have to reflect on the decade before. The 1920s was a time when more people had surplus income. This is especially true for the growing middle class and the rich. It was also a time when people decided to try and make extra money on the financial market. This was exciting because many middle- and working-class people who traded on the financial market in the 1920s would not have thought about stocks and shares in the decades before.

Consumerism had hit the United States in a way that had not happened before. Numerous industries were booming, and people were buying more products than they ever had before. All of these things are normally seen as positive. However, as mentioned in the last chapter, although groups of people had extra income, this was not true for everyone.

Many people and investors spent their money in the stock market, but many of them used money they did not have. Instead of their own cash, they would pay in the form of credit or installments. Must-have products, like radios or washing machines, were often purchased in the same way. When looking back, it is clear to see why the Great Depression happened.

But was the Wall Street Crash really the start of the Great Depression or the catalyst? Many people think the Great Depression happened because of the Wall Street Crash. As the decades have passed, this way of thinking has slowly changed. It is clear, however, that the moment the crash happened, it led to a change in the economy and the lives of Americans.

Hoover Takes Over

On March 4th, 1929, Herbert Hoover was inaugurated as the president of the United States. At this point in the American story, the economy was doing well, purchasing was high, and it was thought that this would continue in an upward direction. Hoover demonstrated the promise America had in his inaugural address:

"Ours is a land rich in resources; stimulating in its glorious beauty; filled with millions of happy homes; blessed with comfort and opportunity. In no nation are the institutions of progress more advanced. In no nation are the fruits of accomplishment more secure. In no nation is the government more worthy of respect. No country is more loved by its people. I have an abiding faith in their capacity, integrity, and high purpose. I have no fears for the future of our country. It is bright with hope."[viii]

Looking at where America was on an economic level, it seemed like the progress would continue or, at the very least, stay in the same place. Sadly, for Hoover and the rest of the American population at the time, this upward trend would not last long.

The Wall Street Crash

The popular saying "what goes up must come down" describes the Wall Street Crash well. As summer was coming to an end in 1929, the prices of stocks and shares began to fall. Because the economy had been so strong, investors in the stock market used that as a reason to buy more stocks. The thought pattern of many people who had previously invested in the market was similar. They saw it as just a bump in the road, believing that the stocks would take a turn in an upward direction soon. These speculations were not anything new. Investors had been speculating without much or any proof at all. The market always corrects itself was the type of advice that was going around at the time.

This time, it was not the case. September saw stocks rise, fall, rise, and then fall again. This time, the prices did not rise again as predicted. Instead, they continued to fall. This brings us to some of the most important dates when talking about the Wall Street Crash: October 24th, October 28th, and October 29th.

On Thursday, October 24th, 1929 (Black Thursday), many people that had bought stocks realized that they might lose what they had invested. The figures from the previous day showed how much money companies had lost. Stock market investors began to panic. Stocks were being sold at a high rate with no one to buy them. In order to calm the frenzy, banks such as J. P. Morgan Jr. of J. P. Morgan & Co. and Albert H. Wiggin of the Chase National Bank decided to invest money into the market by buying shares to relieve the frenzy. This was sadly just a short-term fix.

For some of the population, losing investments in the stock market would have been catastrophic. This was because many stocks and shares had been bought on credit. That meant if their stocks went down, they would have lost the money they invested and would still have to pay back the credit they owed. If they had the money in the first place, they wouldn't have needed to buy stocks in this way.

Monday, October 28th, had a similar story. Headlines such as "Stock Prices in Disastrous Crash" were being printed by newspapers, and stocks fell even lower than the previous Thursday.[ix] By October 29th, the damage was done, and the day known as Black Tuesday had arrived. The stock market took a plunge, and companies dropped drastically. For instance, General Electric and Allied Chemical had lost twenty-eight points and thirty-five points, respectively.[x]

More stocks were being sold at an alarming rate, and the big banks would not be able to fix the problem this time. Over sixteen million shares were traded that day, and the losses from the Wall Street Crash would be felt across the nation and even the world. The losses from October 28th and 29th are recorded as being as high as thirty billion dollars.[xi]

Had it just been the Wall Street Crash, it is possible that the economy would have recovered within a few years. However, the fragility of the world's economy in the 1920s set the stage for the Great Depression.

After the Crash

To make matters worse, the population didn't just panic when it came to selling their stocks and shares. People hurried to the banks, withdrawing their money in a move called a bank run, which led to banks running out of money and needing to close. This led to further panic.

An image of a bank run
https://en.wikipedia.org/wiki/File:American_union_bank.gif

Since America had hit a recession at the beginning of the 1920s and recovered after one and a half years, it is understandable why it was not clear to everyone how grave the situation was. When the post-war recession hit in 1920, the government was able to take a hands-off approach, and the economy still recovered. With this knowledge, many of the upper-class people were not worried about the economy. By looking at the newspapers during the last few days of October 1929, it was clear that a huge event had happened, but it is also clear that the reporters thought it would not last. Newspapers featured stories of the crash, and it was often the main headline. But many newspapers also dedicated a lot of the front page to other stories, such as films that had recently been released and the local news. With that being said, they could not have known that the recession they headed into was what we now know as the Great Depression.

Long-term Effects of the Depression

Some banks that originally closed as a result of the crash were able to open again at a later date, but some never reopened. Banks certainly closed in the 1920s, but it was nothing compared to the number of banks that closed during the Great Depression. In 1931, over eight hundred banks closed during the months of October and November alone. This trend continued as the Depression deepened.

Effects were also felt in other areas of society. Many of those who had bought products using credit were not able to pay their installments. Without getting their normal income from these customers, stores ran into difficulties. Pockets were tight, and spending slowed down. As a result, many stores had to close, and of course, the people that worked in the stores lost their jobs. Unemployment, in general, was at an all-time high, reaching 25 percent at one point. Other industries, such as construction, were affected too. Companies that wanted to do extra building work held on to their money instead of moving forward with building projects.

The rise in unemployment was vast. The unemployed would travel from city to city in the hopes of finding a new job. Since they were unemployed, they couldn't afford the fare and would often travel without a valid ticket. However, it was necessary to travel in this way for such a time as this.

People that still kept their jobs were working on a reduced salary. Most middle- and upper-class families could no longer afford to have "hired help." This resulted in more people losing their jobs. By 1932, almost a quarter of the population was searching for new employment.

Common to any economic recession, suicide rates and the rate of people having mental health problems rose. However, the stories of floods of people throwing themselves off buildings were embellished. Still, Americans did commit suicide in numerous ways. People, including the president of the Rochester Gas and Electric Corporation, felt the burden of the recession and ended their lives. In 1932, over 20.0 of every 100,000 people died this way (suicide statistics are based on every 100,000 people, so you would read this as over 20 people in every 100,000 committed suicide).

Herbert Hoover, who was elected as president eight months before the crash, seemed like the perfect person for the job. Before he was elected president, he had worked in various roles. One of his previous jobs included ensuring Europeans had food during food shortages after the war. He also worked as the secretary of commerce under Warren Harding and under Calvin Coolidge when they were president. Surely someone who had that level of experience would be perfect to lead a nation out of a depression. Unfortunately for Hoover, this is not how many saw him, particularly as the Great Depression deepened. Those opinions are still alive today, as many see him as not doing enough to alleviate the effects.

Hoover wanted to allow the market to correct itself, which, as previously mentioned, was a similar step that the government took during the recession that began in 1920. As you can imagine, this hands-off approach, whether right or wrong, was not welcomed by many. This was especially true in 1932. By this time, the United States was deep into the Depression. People who had lost their income as a result of the Depression had also lost their homes. It is safe to say that many people were unsatisfied with the work Hoover had done. Over

250,000 people lost their homes in 1932 alone. The general population was so unhappy that many of them even named their new homes, which were self-made shelters, after him, calling their shantytowns Hoovervilles.

Dealing with the Great Depression would have been tough enough, but the problems for the country and for Hoover didn't stop there. The soil in the farming states of New Mexico, Texas, Nebraska, Kansas, Colorado, and Oklahoma was affected by dust storms.

An image of a dust storm in Texas
https://en.wikipedia.org/wiki/File:Dust_storm_approaching_Stratford,_Texas_1935.jpg

The storms happened as a result of over-farming and drought, and they lasted for the majority of the decade. This is commonly known as the Dust Bowl. Storms created by the dry soil were so severe that they would cause darkness during the day, affecting the population in numerous ways. Americans covered their windows and doors with clothes to prevent the dust from entering their homes. This was somewhat effective, but the dust was often still found in homes. The storms also caused health problems like asthma and pneumonia. The most severe storm happened on April 14th, 1935. During this time, approximately three hundred million tons of topsoil generated a storm in the area.

With the loss of jobs and savings from the Great Depression, farmers were unable to cope with the situation created by the Dust Bowl. The storms made the soil unfarmable, causing mass migrations to places like California.

One of the most famous images of the Great Depression, Migrant Mother by Dorothea Lange

This image is available from the United States Library of Congress's Prints and Photographs division under the digital ID fsa.8b29516; https://en.wikipedia.org/wiki/File:Lange-MigrantMother02.jpg

Hoover did try to help the economy by passing the Smoot-Hawley Tariff Act. This law meant that foreign imports would be taxed higher than products made in America. The law specified that this would affect products that could be bought in America instead. The aim was to help American businesses. Sadly, this law is commonly seen as one of the reasons why the Great Depression lasted for so long in America. It encouraged countries like Canada to change their own import law and put a higher tax on American imports to Canada. Hoover also ensured money went back into the economy by helping to pass legislation, which enabled banks in trouble to be bailed out during his last year as president.

Hoover's failures during the Great Depression made a huge percentage of the population want a different type of leader. Many Americans wanted a leader that was proactive. They wanted a leader who could help the nation.

Needless to say, Hoover did not win the next election. Instead, Franklin Delano Roosevelt (FDR) won the election in 1932. When campaigning, Roosevelt spoke about a New Deal, which was his plan to help America out of the Great Depression. Roosevelt promised the nation that he would be the president they needed. Within his first one hundred days, Roosevelt began to fulfill his promise of a New Deal for America. He was the first president to carry out a massive amount of work in the first one hundred days of his presidency, which has since become a tradition and continues even to this day.[xii]

Roosevelt ordered a bank holiday in order to calm the market down and discover which banks should remain solvent. He also created an organization called the Civilian Conservation Corps (CCC). This corporation employed young people from the ages of eighteen to twenty-five. A key job that the CCC had involved the Dust Bowl. The corps was given the role of planting trees to improve the soil in the Dust Bowl areas. The planting of trees, as well as better weather conditions, helped to resolve the dust storms. The CCC also served as another form of employment for those who were in need of work during the Great Depression.

Roosevelt also communicated with the public through his famous Fireside Chats. This was a radio broadcast where he spoke about the current economic situation. Roosevelt was a president who seemed proactive and visible.

But just like with every president, there were supporters and opponents. With that being said, the common consensus then and even when looking back now is that Roosevelt was a good and popular president. He was the only president to be elected four times; the US government put term limits on the presidency shortly after FDR died, so this is no longer possible. FDR was likely popular for his actions to solve the Great Depression, and people hoped that proactiveness would extend to World War II as well.

After the attack on Pearl Harbor on December 7th, 1941, America joined the fight in the Second World War, which had begun in 1939. As a result, many people went to fight against the Nazis and the Japanese army. Due to this, the unemployment rate dropped, which had risen during the recession of 1937. Although there are differing opinions, it is argued that the Great Depression ended once the war began. Some economists and historians believe the Depression did not finish until the war was won.[xiii] Regardless of one's stance, it is clear that as a result of the US joining the war, unemployment dropped. It helped the economy leave the Great Depression behind.

The Great Depression brought about a time of desperation in America. The poor who had already been struggling in the 1920s were hit hard. It led many people to lose their jobs and struggle to find new ones. The Wall Street Crash was a pinnacle moment. Although it was not the only cause of the Great Depression worldwide, it marked the beginning of the Depression in the United States. FDR's leadership and the Second World War helped America move out of the financial crisis and into a new era.

Chapter 3 – America Joins the War

By the end of the 1930s, most of the countries in the world had suffered from the effects of the Great Depression, and the nations were all in the rebuilding phase. Prior to that, the United States had lost many young people in WWI and had decided to look after itself instead of reaching out to help countries on the other side of the ocean.

Germany's economic problem after WWI led to the rise of an oppressive leader called Adolf Hitler. Hitler had decided to stretch his hand outside of Germany, and as a result, the Nazis invaded Austria in 1938. The Nazis invaded Czechoslovakia and Poland in 1939, the latter resulting in the start of WWII. The US government had to decide what to do. Should they leave the Europeans to fight THEIR war, or should they get involved in a war that would cost more American lives?

So, why did the US join World War Two?

After the casualties and deaths that the First World War brought, many Americans were united and did not want to fight in another war. In the minds of the Americans, World War Two was a European problem. With Europe being so far away from the States, it is easy to see why so many of the population held that point of view. What changed the perspective of the Americans, and why did it change so quickly? A quick answer to those questions is the attack on Pearl Harbor. The attack changed the US perception of the war. Before Pearl Harbor, not only did the population not want to enter the war, but Roosevelt also did not force the issue. That was, of course, until December 7th, 1941.

Until that time, the US had played a role in the war that did not involve combat. From the winter of 1939 until late January 1942, America had supplied France, Britain, and other Allied nations with weaponry and resources. The United States continued to supply resources to the British and other Allies when they did not have enough money to pay for them through the LEND-LEASE ACT.[xiv] Roosevelt knew that as important as money was (and naturally still is), he needed to continue to help the Allies fight the Nazis.

Before WWII started, Japan had been at war with China. They had been at war since July 7th, 1937. This worried the US government, and it tried to put pressure on Japan by cutting off resources like oil. Oil was, of course, an important resource, and most of the oil that Japan imported was from the United States.

However, this action from the Americans did not help to quell international relations. Hideki Tojo was originally the military leader in Japan, and he became the prime minister in 1941. He wanted Asia to belong to its people but more specifically to Japan. Indonesia, which was then called the Dutch Indies, was ruled by Holland. The Philippines had American naval bases on it. And the French had been ruling over Indochina since the late 1800s. The restrictions from the Americans, plus the Europeanization and colonization that had occurred in Asia, made Hideki Tojo want to make a drastic change. On top of this, during this period of time, Japan saw itself as the most superior nation on Earth.

Hideki Tojo decided he needed to create a plan to strike the United States. This plan ended up involving Pearl Harbor. The brain behind the operation was Admiral Isoroku Yamamoto. He created a plan that could have devastated the American military.

The plan was to carry out an air and sea attack on an American naval base. The US Navy was already stationed at Pearl Harbor; it had been used as a naval base since 1899. In fact, the troops had once staged a drill in 1933 to simulate an attack; it did not go well. The Japanese military leaders had decided to attack the United States in a way that would disable it and keep it out of the war.

By the time the Japanese military had formed the plan, the US military knew that Japan was going to attack one of their bases. Thus, their bases were on alert. It was assumed that a US base in Asia was going to be attacked; however, they soon found out that their estimation was incorrect.

On December 7th, 1941, Japanese airplanes and submarines were in the vicinity of Pearl Harbor. By the time the Japanese military started to attack, it was too late for the Americans. Most of their airplanes were parked on the runway. This was initially done just in case there was an attack so they could take off quickly. However, parking the airplanes on the runway left the American military unable to fight back since the Japanese forces shot at the planes, rendering them unusable. They then moved to attack the battleships, which were also attacked by Japanese midget submarines. The attack lasted around two hours, but it resulted in the deaths of almost 2,500 Americans. Battleships were damaged and destroyed, and more than three hundred aircraft were destroyed too.[xv] However, the attack did not debilitate the American military as much as the Japanese had planned.

An image of the USS Arizona after the attack on Pearl Harbor. Almost half of the people who died in the Pearl Harbor attack were on this battleship

https://en.wikipedia.org/wiki/File:The_USS_Arizona_(BB-39)_burning_after_the_Japanese_attack_on_Pearl_Harbor_-_NARA_195617_-_Edit.jpg

The day after the attack, Roosevelt addressed Congress to discuss the "dastardly attack" and to ask if the United States could join the war.[xvi] This was America's entrance to WWII, as the politicians decided to declare war on Japan. A few days later, Germany, which was allies with Japan, declared war on the US.

The events of Pearl Harbor triggered American citizens and made them want to join the war. Over 2,500 people applied to join the US Armed Forces just days after the attack.[xvii] The attack also had a negative impact on some of the citizens. Citizens and immigrants who were Japanese or had a Japanese background were treated terribly by much of the population. They were also rounded up and placed in internment camps. About 120,000 people, most of whom were US citizens, were forced to live in these camps. There were also camps for German and Italian Americans, as well as people from other Axis nations, although their numbers pale in comparison to the Japanese Americans.

Winston Churchill, Prime Minister of Britain, was relieved that the US had decided to join the war. France had already been taken over by the Nazis at the beginning of the summer of 1940, and Britain was in need of support. The British, with the help of their colonies, were busy fighting in Europe. They were also fighting Germany's allies, the Italians. Fighting was also taking place in North Africa. A place of interest for the British was Egypt, as they wanted to keep control of the Suez Canal. The British were worried that their oil supply in the Middle East was going to be taken over by their enemies. This meant fighting was taking place on numerous fronts.

Up until the United States joined the war, Britain was able to hold on because it still had an empire. Britain had people from countries like Jamaica and India fighting in a military capacity. Britain also used the empire to provide the war effort with supplies. The Soviet Union, which was originally a German ally, began to fight on the side of the Allies after being attacked by the Germans in June 1941. However, by December 8th, it became clear that with the British Empire, the Soviet Union, and the United States on its side, the Allies might actually be able to win the war.

Since the war was geographically complex, the United States entering the conflict was not a sure fix. Initially, Franklin Delano Roosevelt and his military commanders wanted to fight the Nazis directly in Europe. In the end, US troops joined the British and some French resistors in North Africa. This section of the war went on until 1943 and ended with the surrender of the German army. This victory for the Allies was important, but there was still more work to be done. The fighting in Europe had been going on simultaneously with fighting in the Pacific, in which the US played an important role, and Churchill and Roosevelt had to create a plan to invade France in order to reach Germany. The Soviet Union also needed help since it had been fighting the Germans on the Eastern Front. They were hoping this would become slightly easier if the Germans had to focus more troops on the Western Front.

D-Day

The British and American military had planned to attack France so they could get soldiers on the ground. The importance of this invasion meant that the Allies knew they had to keep the details of it under wraps. An invasion had occurred in August 1942, which only led to a terrible loss. The Allies knew they needed a win here. Their next invasion had to be successful.

The Germans knew through the intelligence they had received that the Allies were planning to attack again. They predicted this was going to happen at Calais, and the majority of the soldiers on board the Allied ships to France thought this too. However, the military ships took an unexpected redirection and headed toward Normandy.

The commanding officers planned five different locations for the Allied armies to land. As the ships headed toward Normandy, the strong winds and unclear sky worked well for the Allies; it was almost as if they had always planned it to be this way. The bad weather covered the multitude of ships heading toward France, which were only revealed once the sky began to clear. This, coupled with the German forces believing they were going to be attacked at another location, greatly helped the Allies. Dummies on parachutes, as well as a fake army at Calais, helped to disorientate the German army and allowed the Allies to carry out their plan.

The Germans had to mobilize their strongest forces to Normandy. Despite the terrible casualties and deaths that the Allies endured, in particular, on their landing on Omaha Beach, the Allies successfully landed on French soil. From this point on, the Allies fought the Germans, taking territory bit by bit in France until Paris was liberated in August 1944.

An image of American troops on their way to Omaha Beach
https://en.wikipedia.org/wiki/File:Approaching_Omaha.jpg

D-Day and the victory in North Africa were important wins for the Allies. However, there is still much to be discussed regarding their victory in the war.

Yalta and Tehran

Post-war Germany was discussed at the Yalta Conference in February 1945. Joseph Stalin, Winston Churchill, and Franklin D. Roosevelt looked at how Germany would be governed after the Allies' victory.

This was not the first conference the leaders had together. Germany had been discussed by the three leaders at the Tehran Conference as well. This took place in November 1943 and lasted for four days. The leaders had discussed the need to invade France, which had surrendered to the Germans three years before. They discussed the coordination of the invasion, in particular how it would work with the fight the Soviets were involved in over on the eastern side of Europe. It was clear the leaders did not agree on what should happen to Germany should they win the war.

So, let's fast forward back to the Yalta Conference in 1945, as it was there that the discussion about post-war Germany resumed. The three leaders decided that Germany needed to be divided, as well as Berlin itself. It was decided at the conference that the Soviet Union would begin to fight against the Japanese army. The leaders planned the Soviet Union's involvement, which would begin in earnest when the European theater had ended.

The politics had been discussed, but the final part of the war in Europe had to be dealt with. After the success of D-Day, it was pretty clear that an Allied victory was imminent, although there were many other factors that played into their success.

The Allies carried out a bombing offense in Dresden, making sure its communication center was out of action. The attack was carried out by the British and the American air forces. The bombing killed up to twenty-five thousand citizens and destroyed over a thousand acres.[xviii]

The Allies had successfully bombed an important city and continued to advance toward the German capital. On their way to the capital, Allied armies found concentration and death camps, revealing the depth of tragedy that had occurred in Germany and the surrounding areas. It is estimated that between five to seven million Jews alone were murdered during World War II, in addition to millions of other minorities and persecuted groups, such as Soviet prisoners of war, ethnic Poles, and the Roma people.

The Allies then began to race to capture the city of Berlin. It was originally agreed at the Yalta Conference that Stalin's army would carry out most of the fighting in Berlin. Although this was agreed upon, when the British and American military got to the western side of Germany, they seemed to be racing to capture the capital as well.

While the war was going on, the public got the news that the US president, who had led them out of the Great Depression and toward a possible win in the war, had died. President Franklin Delano Roosevelt died on April 12th, 1945, less than a month before Germany surrendered. Vice President Harry S. Truman took over the role of president.

Meanwhile, in the race toward Berlin, the Soviet Union got there first, taking approximately 1.5 million soldiers to secure the capital. The battle started on April 16th. By April 30th, Hitler knew the war was lost and committed suicide. The battle led to the surrender of Germany, which happened on May 7th, 1945.

Just over a month later, on June 26th, most of the countries that fought with the Allies had signed an international charter solidifying the need for an international body that fought for peace. Since then, that has been one of the main purposes of the United Nations. This peace organization would officially come into being later that same year in October. Today, it continues to promote harmony between the countries of the world and ensure nations do not violate human rights. It has come under criticism for being too heavy-handed in wars and for engaging in corruption, but many view the organization in a positive light.

On July 17th, 1945, the three leaders of the Soviet Union, the United States, and Britain met again for the Potsdam Conference. The conference lasted until August 2nd. This time, there was a change in personnel. Truman had taken the role of president of the United States, and Clement Attlee joined just over a week after the conference started because he had become the prime minister of Britain. Stalin wasn't overjoyed with this change. The leaders met to continue the conversation about the division of Germany and reparations for the Soviet Union. Furthermore, the three leaders discussed plans for denazification.

Although the war had been won in north Africa and Europe, it was not over. There was still another major Axis power on the field: Japan. The US had been fighting the Japanese since 1942. They had managed to take over land that the Japanese had occupied, and the US Army was slowly moving toward Japan. The continual battle with Japan was also discussed at the conference. The leaders discussed the terms they needed in order to win the war. One of those terms was an unconditional surrender from Japan.

The Potsdam conference was important because just before the conference, it was communicated to Truman that the atomic bomb, which a team of scientists had been working on since 1941, had finally worked.

The Manhattan project was aimed at creating a weapon to use on Germany in WWII. The us government was warned that the Germans could also be working on an atomic weapon. With help from the British, the American government had chosen to try to create one of their own.

The bomb was tested at several sites, and in July 1945, in New Mexico, the first atomic bomb was successfully tested. Although the war with the Germans was over, Truman was aware that the bomb could be used elsewhere.

The US carried out a magnitude of bombing raids over Japan, although these were not on an atomic level yet. The bombing of Tokyo in March 1945 is just an example. It caused fires to break out, which destroyed most of the area. Approximately 100,000 people died as a result.[xix] Despite this, the Japanese refused to surrender.

President Truman, along with his advisors, thought the atomic bomb could be used to make the Japanese government surrender. They warned the Japanese government that they should surrender to avoid life-threatening consequences.

The surrender did not occur after the Potsdam Conference as the US government had demanded, so the US decided dropping the atomic bombs would be the right move to force Japan to surrender. Regardless of which side you stood on back then, it was clear the bombs would create sheer havoc. The test of the bomb in New Mexico led many of the scientists involved in the project to speak out against dropping the bombs and even signed a petition against it.[xx]

Despite this, on July 6th, 1945, an atomic bomb was dropped on Hiroshima, which instantly killed over eighty thousand people. This does not account for the deaths that took place afterward as a direct result of the bombing; it is hard to put a precise number of the causalities of these bombs because many died after the fact due to cancer, birth defects, and brain issues. Two days later, as discussed at Yalta in February of that year, the Soviet Union attacked Japan. Since Japan had yet to surrender, the US dropped another bomb on Japan a day later, hitting Nagasaki.

Many question if the second bomb was even needed, considering the vast majority of those killed had been civilians. Regardless of what one thinks of the atomic bombs, the series of events led to the Japanese government deciding to surrender on August 15th, 1945, with the official signing taking place on September 2nd. The war was finally over. Although President Truman had told the world his military had used an atomic bomb after the incident on August 6th, the true devastation of both bombs was not made public and would not be made public until the 1970s.

WWII saw the Allies fighting against a European leader who had oppressed many and had tried to take over much of Europe, either by conquest or through allying with them. The Allies worked together to win the war on multiple fronts and continents. Although the Allies are seen as the winners of the war, it is clear that huge losses occurred on both sides. Bombing raids and combat killed citizens and soldiers, and between forty to eighty-five million people died during WWII (there is a huge discrepancy since it is hard to know just how many civilians died). Huge cities like Dresden and Tokyo no longer looked the same. France and Britain struggled after the war, and Germany was occupied by the Allies. The effects of the war resulted in a change in power that led to the next stage of war: the Cold War.

Chapter 4 – The Cold War: Beginning and Escalation

After the War

WWII shaped the world in more ways than one. The British Empire was falling apart. The British had committed an extreme number of resources to defeat the Germans and could no longer hold onto their empire as they had before.

Additionally, Britain and France, which were once seen as powerful nations, were bearing the burden of bombing raids and trying to rebuild after the war. After mostly recovering from WWI, not to mention the effects of the Great Depression, the burden of WWII was just too high for many.

Germany was also bomb-stricken and suffering in more ways than one. Instead of just losing the land it had conquered both before and during the war, it was also divided into four occupational zones. Japan, which had also been a powerful nation before the war, saw loss and ruin like no other.

Due to the devastation, there were only two nations that were still going strong, in one way or another.

Two Superpowers

Out of the most powerful countries in the world, the only two that were strong enough in the eyes of the world and in reality were the Soviet Union and America.

Except for the attack on Pearl Harbor, the United States was left without the reality of the war that Europe and Asia had faced. They didn't have to rebuild major cities like the rest of the Allies and the Axis powers. America was still a wealthy nation, and at the end of the war, it had arisen as a new superpower.

The Soviet Union's story was quite different. Battles like the Battle of Stalingrad caused many casualties and the need to rebuild areas that were completely destroyed. Around twenty-seven million Russians died in the war, although the number is still being debated. Regardless of the debate, it is believed the Soviet Union lost the most people of any nation in WWII. Although the reality was harsh, the Soviet Union (also known as the USSR) gained something the other countries did not: a lot of territories. Their army had pushed the Nazis back into Berlin, liberating the countries that the Germans had taken over. By May 1945, the Soviet Union had occupied the countries that surrounded it on its western side.

This means that by the end of the war, there were two countries that emerged more powerful than before: the Soviet Union and the United States. These nations became known as the world's superpowers.

The Superpowers and the Cold War

Having two superpowers is not necessarily a bad thing. The only problem was they had huge differences.

The leaders in the United States believed in the ideology of capitalism, which is often strongly linked with democracy. The leaders in the Soviet Union believed in the ideology of communism.

The Soviet Union had become a communist country after Russia's revolution in 1917. This scared many Americans because a revolution is never carried out peacefully, and stories coming out of the Soviet Union led to the Red Scare in America, which took place from 1917 to 1920. A red scare can be described as a nation being scared of communist ideas taking root and changing society as they know it. A red scare typically consists of the media portraying communists in a particularly negative way, which often scares the public. It also involves police raids in order to arrest suspected communists. It is similar to how many countries have viewed Islamic extremists over the past twenty years. The negative perception people had of communism lingered in America, so it was definitely still on people's minds after the end of World War II.

In 1945, a communist country had taken over territories from the Nazis. This concerned many Americans. Harry Truman, who was president at the time, believed something needed to be done to stop communism from spreading across the world, and he was not alone in thinking this.

But how did the Soviet Union get so big? To understand how this happened, we have to jump back to 1941. Joseph Stalin was warned that Hitler's army would attack the Soviet Union in 1941; however, he did not believe his spies' reports. Although this might sound strange, it makes sense in a way because the Soviet Union and Germany had signed a non-aggression pact and were on the same side at the time. What Stalin did not know was that Hitler wanted the very resources the Soviets had been providing Germany. Instead of Hitler receiving it from Stalin, he wanted the resources to be completely at his disposal, so he decided to ignore the pact the two leaders had made.

While Stalin was the leader of the Soviet Union, his country was attacked by the Germans. This was not the first time that this had happened. Germany had attacked Russia in WWI too. Stalin decided it was time to protect his country. He wanted to create a "buffer zone" around the Soviet Union to stop an attack like this from ever happening again. Keeping control of the countries around him gave him the buffer zone he was looking for.

WWII left Europe in a desolate place. Not only were buildings and cities destroyed, but so was the economy. The leaders in the Western world feared that if things continued in this way, it would cause people to think about a change in how their country was run. One of these changes could be embracing communism. Countries like France and Britain had no way to prevent this possible worldview change from happening on their own. However, they had one of the two superpowers on their side, and the superpower seemingly came to the rescue in the form of two plans: the Truman Doctrine and the Marshall Plan.

The Truman Doctrine was introduced in Truman's speech in March 1947. It became clear that America had chosen to fight against communism in a military capacity. The Marshall Plan extended the Truman Doctrine even further.

Similar to how America aided the Allies in WWII against the threat of the Nazis, the Marshall Plan aided those against another threat. This time, it was the threat of communism. The Marshall Plan saw the United States promise to send aid to a country that had financial needs. Due to the dire state many countries were in as a result of the war, the plan was costly, and America ended up sending over ten billion dollars to countries around the world. Of course, the US government hoped that sending this financial aid would prevent people from rebelling and toppling governments to welcome a dictator. The US was worried that a repeat of the events of 1917 in Russia would happen in a country even closer to home.

Anti-Communism

The US government was not alone in halting the threat of communism, however real that threat might have been. Like in 1917, a red scare happened once again in the United States, and it flared up in the late 1940s. Led by Senator Joseph McCarthy, a hunt for communists on American soil began. Many government workers were accused of being communists and were investigated. But it did not stop there. People in a range of industries, such as education, journalism, and entertainment, were accused, and many lost their jobs. It led to a change in American culture. People were scared to share their views just in case they were accused of being a communist. Fear changed the way people interacted with others, leading to relationships being shattered among friends and family members.

Meanwhile, the Soviet Union was seemingly expanding, which only added to the fear the Western world had about the expansion of communism. The Soviet Union had forced the German army back to Berlin and liberated the countries the Nazis had taken over.

However, the liberated countries did not feel liberated at all. Instead of the liberated countries going back to life like it was before the war, they were guided by the Soviet Union's policies. Stalin had allowed communism's influence to spread beyond the Soviet Union's borders by influencing elections and making sure governments were run in a manner he saw fit. His vision of having a buffer zone around the Soviet Union was being realized.

It became clear that there was a divide in Europe between the West and the East. The East was commonly known as the Eastern Bloc. The divide became even clearer once NATO (North Atlantic Treaty Organization) was created in 1949. NATO was formed when a group of countries decided to be military allies after the war and defend each other when needed. NATO was initially made up of twelve nations, including the United States, France, and the United Kingdom. To intensify the divide between the West and the East, West Germany was introduced to NATO in 1955. The Soviet Union then formed its own military alliance called the Warsaw Pact in May of that year, which included East Germany. Actions during this time made the unification of Germany even more tricky than it was before.

The Arms Race Begins

The Cold War brought more than a fight between two different ideologies. It brought a race to create the most powerful weapons.

WWII saw the use of weapons that the world had not seen before. The Americans had tested and used nuclear bombs on Japan. The use of the bombs made the Soviets distrust the Americans. This was because the US government did not reveal its plans to use a bomb of that magnitude in WWII, just that it was "a new weapon of unusual destructive force." Although Stalin knew about the information due to his spies, he did not trust Truman since he did not tell him about his plans for the bombs. They were, after all, on the same side at that point. The Soviet Union used the end of the war as an opportunity to develop its arms too, and by the end of the 1940s, it had its own nuclear bombs.

An arms race between these two nations had begun. Only three years later, in 1952, the United States showed it was not ready to concede, as it had developed a hydrogen bomb, which is more destructive than an atomic bomb. In 1955, the Soviet Union showed that it was a worthy competitor, as it had produced its own hydrogen bomb. Both countries tried to outdo each other by producing the best weapons. This only made the events in the coming decades all the scarier.

The War in Korea

Out of all of the wars in the modern age, the Korean War is the one that many, looking back, see as useless. As a result of World War Two, Korea was split into two parts separated by the 38th parallel. Stalin's army occupied the northern part, and Truman's army occupied the South. Both of the superpowers assumed Korea would reunite. They placed a leader in their own halves until the reunification happened, allowing their troops to vacate Korea when the time came.

Kim Il-Sung became the leader of the North, and Syngman Rhee became the leader of the South. Both leaders were also hoping for reunification but in a different way than many hoped. In order to unify Korea, after a while of petitioning support from Stalin, Kim Il-Sung's army stormed the South. A war occurring so close to WWII was frightening for many in the world. Even though many did not know the true devastation of the bombing of Hiroshima and Nagasaki, practically everyone knew that the United States had war technology that had never been seen or used before. Since the Soviet Union had been developing its own weapons technology, this new war worried many.

Kim Il-Sung believed invading the South was the only way to reunite Korea. North Korea invaded the South in June 1950, and within a week, it had captured land in the South, including Seoul. To make matters worse for the South Korean army, some of their members joined the other side. From North Korea's perspective, it was a good start to the war. Kim Il-Sung did not believe the war would last all that long, especially since things were going according to his plan.

The US supported the South Korean army by sending troops to fight against the North. Based on the Americans' fears and policies at the time, fighting in the war was important to make sure the whole of Korea did not become a communist country. They had to stop the spread of communism.

Thus, the US supported the South, and the Soviet Union supported the communist North. The war became the first proxy war between the two superpowers. They were fighting for their side, as well as their ideology.

Despite North Korea's seemingly inevitable victory, as the North Korean army was doing well at the beginning of the war, it did not stay that way. South Korea's army began to make gains four months later and took back some of the lands that had been captured.

By the time both sides agreed to negotiate, both armies were back on their side of the 38th parallel. South Korea had been bombed, cities ceased to exist, and yet nothing had truly been achieved. Dwight D. Eisenhower, who became president in 1953, used the war to get elected. He showed voters during the election campaign that he was ready to find a resolution to end the war. His arguments had credibility since he was a general. An armistice was signed in 1953; however, it was not all Eisenhower's doing.

The death of Stalin helped put an end to the war too, and the Soviet government now wanted to end the war in Korea. As of January 2022, the countries are still at war since no treaty has ever been signed. In 1953, though, the countries agreed to stop fighting each other, but clashes between the two still occur today.

The Space Race

The competition between the two superpowers had many levels, and it took to the skies and beyond that too. Both the Soviet Union and the United States were interested in sending satellites into space. This original idea developed into a race that the world had never seen before. What started as launching satellites into space became a competition of great proportions.

Four days into October 1957 saw the Soviet Union take a huge step in the direction of winning the Space Race. They had successfully launched their satellite, famously known as Sputnik, into space. Although the US launched a satellite about four months later, the Soviet Union was in the lead. Many believe the US won since it was the first to send a human to the moon by the end of the 1960s. This race continued alongside two other events that could have changed the world, although it certainly impacted the countries involved.

An image of Buzz Aldrin on the moon
https://en.wikipedia.org/wiki/File:Aldrin_Apollo_11_original.jpg.

The Berlin Wall

After WWII, Germany was divided into four parts. Britain, the Soviet Union, the United States, and France each occupied a part. Berlin was also divided and occupied by each of the countries. This was supposed to be a temporary measure until Germany was reunited again. Each part was run separately, but the US and Britain realized that, economically, it was better to work together, and they joined their parts together on January 1ˢᵗ, 1947. France then joined them in 1949.

This meant the Western part of Germany was occupied by the three democratic countries, and the East was occupied by the Soviet Union. This did not help to reunify Germany; it actually became clear that the issue of reunification was going to be harder than first believed. Germany was not officially reunited until after the Berlin Wall came down at the end of the 1980s. The wall was built to solve a problem.

By the end of WWII, many people were leaving to go to the West. Around 200,000 people left East Germany to go to the West in 1960 alone.[xxi] Berlin's location made this easy to do because it was easy to travel around, despite the fact that it was run by different powers.

Walter Ulbricht, who was the head of the Council of State in East Germany, had a solution to the problem. He sent plans to Nikita Khrushchev, the leader of the USSR from 1953 to 1964, regarding building a wall to stop the flow of people moving to the Western side of Germany. Walter Ulbricht had declared to the German people that a wall would not be built. Despite this declaration, during the early morning of August 13th, 1961, a wall was constructed to divide Berlin.

The original construction of the wall was made of barbed wire. However, as more and more people tried to escape from one side of Berlin to the other, the wall was adapted to stop this. The barbed wire was slowly replaced with concrete, and it eventually included an inner wall to prevent people from escaping.

The wall led to another moment after WWII where the world thought WWIII could begin. On October 27th, 1961, an American officer was denied entry to East Berlin at Checkpoint Charlie. It escalated, and tanks from both sides faced each other in a standoff. One false move from a soldier and more than an international incident could have happened. This standoff lasted for twenty-four hours and had the world on edge. Little did everyone know that the world would be on edge again exactly 365 days later.

Cuba

In 1959, the revolution in Cuba finally ended. Fidel Castro and his organization had taken control of Cuba. The revolution happened as a result of the corruption that was happening in Cuba. The rich were getting richer, and America was profiting from the Cuban economy. When Castro took over Cuba, he nationalized farms and banks and tried to make changes to benefit the Cuban people. Maybe that was one of the reasons why Eisenhower, who was president at the time, avoided meeting Castro when he visited the United States, as America could no longer profit from Cuba in the way it had before. Castro was not a democratic leader, and he got rid of anyone who did not support him, many of whom escaped to America. Worried that Castro was a communist (at this time, he did not consider himself to be one), the US Central Intelligence Agency (the CIA) tried to assassinate Castro a number of times.

The Bay of Pigs

Before John F. Kennedy became president, Eisenhower had signed off on a plan to overthrow Castro by using many of the people who had escaped Cuba. By the time the plan was ready, JFK was in power, and he allowed the plan to go ahead. The original plan was to invade the island and overthrow Castro's government.

However, the plan went terribly wrong. Castro found out about the plan, and when the makeshift army landed in Cuba, the Cuban army was ready for them. The American army, which was meant to help the Cuban exiles who had infiltrated Cuba, backed out at the last minute, worried that the world would see them as bullies.

The Cuban Missile Crisis

With the assassination attempts and the Bay of Pigs incident, Castro decided it was time to get some support. He turned to the Soviet Union and officially declared that Cuba was a communist state. The Soviet Union decided to help and sent missiles to Cuba. These missiles were seen as a way to protect Cuba from its neighbor to the north. It also benefited the Soviet Union since it meant that the United States had missiles pointing at them from only ninety miles away.

In the age of espionage, spy planes were flying over Cuba and spotted missiles being installed. All of this led to the Cuban Missile Crisis.

To avoid a military conflict, Kennedy issued a quarantine on any ships that were on their way to Cuba. The days of negotiation between Kennedy and Khrushchev were tense, to say the least. It could have ended up in a war if the leaders did not negotiate their way out of the situation. This was especially true after a US airplane was shot down on October 27ᵗʰ, 1962, resulting in the only death of the Cuban Missile Crisis. It had the world on edge. Would the US retaliate against the USSR for killing one of their men? However, the United States and the Soviet Union wanted to find a path that would avoid another world war. As a result, the Soviet Union agreed to remove its missiles from Cuba. Although this next piece of news was not disclosed to the public, the US agreed to remove its missiles that were in close proximity to the Soviet Union.

The beginning of the Cold War saw the US pitted against the Soviet Union. The differing ideologies led to a number of incidents, including the standoff at the checkpoint at the Berlin Wall and the Cuban Missile Crisis. These two superpowers also used their influence to allow their military to engage in a proxy war. Sadly, the war in Korea would not be the only proxy war in which the two nations would take part.

Chapter 5 – Vietnam: A Divided Nation

When most people talk about the Vietnam War, they often describe the difficulty the US Army had when fighting over there. People also talk about the tactics both sides used during combat. Although these topics are key talking points when discussing the war, it is important to know there is more to the war than many people talk about or even know.

Like many nations in Africa and Asia, Vietnam's fortune was affected by one simple thing: colonization. In the 1800s, the French government was trying to make its mark on the world by expanding its empire, and they took over the areas of the world that we know as Vietnam, Laos, and Cambodia. This area of the world was called Indochina.

Some Vietnamese citizens capitalized on the French taking over and profited from embracing the changes they made. Many of the rich used French colonization as an opportunity to get a French education. As you can imagine, a huge number of the Vietnamese people did the opposite, and uprisings happened during this time, but they did not materialize into anything major.

The Effects of World War II

During WWII, the French had bigger problems than controlling parts of their empire. France was overrun by the Germans in 1940. At that moment in time, Japan was taking over the colonies that the British and French had occupied in Southeast Asia. As a result of France's surrender to Germany, it did not have firm control of Indochina. Japan used that to try to take complete control of the area.

Japan's move to take over countries in Asia happened for various reasons. The Japanese leader, Hideki Tojo, saw that much of Asia was colonized by people who were not from Asia. This angered him, and he wanted to change this. Furthermore, when the US prevented Japan from gaining resources like oil, he realized this was his chance to take over the colonies and gain resources for his nation.

There were a few things that could have happened in Vietnam after WWII. One of the possibilities lay in the hands of French-educated Ho Chi Minh. He was Vietnamese and was previously exiled by the French. When Japan took over Vietnam in 1940, Ho Chi Minh knew this was the opportunity he and the Vietnamese people needed to gain their freedom. He became the leader of the Viet Minh, the group that sought Vietnamese independence from outside forces, including Japan.

Ho Chi Minh returned to Vietnam and revived the Viet Minh in 1941. Supported by the Americans, he and the Viet Minh fought the Japanese to ensure they did not gain control of the whole country. When Japan lost WWII, Ho Chi Minh and the Viet Minh had already received lots of support from the Vietnamese people. With the backing from the people, he would have been a possible leader for the country after the war.

The other group that could have run Vietnam after the war was the French government. After the war, the members of the French government made it clear they wanted to take back their colony and "refused to let go" of it.[xxii]

The two possibilities occurred simultaneously. It resulted in the French taking control of much of the southern part of Vietnam and the Viet Minh taking control of much of the northern part. Naturally, this situation did not stay peaceful and created yet another war.

War Again?

This war was puzzling to many French citizens. They had a fresh taste of their country being taken over in WWII, and the citizens did not understand why their country would continue to do the same to another.

Like most of Europe, the French were depleted after WWII and needed support to resecure what they saw as their territory. Fighting a war against the Vietnamese army was on a level of difficulty that they could not have imagined. It involved guerrilla warfare, fighting in rivers, and being involved in battles whilst dealing with torrential weather conditions. The French looked to their allies for help.

When the US government decided the Vietnamese figure they had supported in WWII to rid of the Japanese army was now a foe, they decided it was the right idea to support the French. The Viet Minh were communists, and the Americans had promised to support countries that were under the threat of communism. As a result, they began to give France weapons, supplying them with over twenty-one thousand tons of weaponry per quarter.

Three years after the war in Vietnam started, there was a turning point. China, which had become a communist nation in 1949, began to support the Viet Minh by sending weapons and advisors to Vietnam. The Viet Minh also had support from the Soviet Union.

Despite the American support, the French forces failed to hold on to the territory they had regained after the war. They suffered a major loss in the Battle of Dien Bien Phu, and after this, they surrendered and lost their colony. The war in Vietnam took a short pause in 1954, but this did not last long.

The Geneva Conference

In 1954, after France had surrendered, the Geneva Conference took place. It took place to discuss the future of Vietnam. It was decided that the country would be divided on the 17th parallel. Like the war in the previous chapter, it was assumed this was going to be a temporary measure.

After the conference, Ngo Dinh Diem became the emperor of the southern part of Vietnam. The South was known as the Republic of Vietnam. Despite his dubious character, he was supported by the American government. The North was still run by Ho Chi Minh and the Viet Minh.

This was not the end of the story for Vietnam. Both territories were run by authoritarian figures who killed people who had differing beliefs from theirs.

Gulf of Tonkin

Although the US had troops and advisors in Vietnam, they were not officially at war. The US had sent troops to Vietnam to support the French, and it just kept troops in the area. The official US involvement began after the Gulf of Tonkin incident.

US ships were stationed at the Gulf of Tonkin. It was originally said that a ship that belonged to the US military was fired at by boats from the North Vietnamese army. This incident happened at the beginning of August 1964. The military also stated that two days later, on August 4th, a second ship was also fired at by the North Vietnamese military.

Information about both ships being fired upon was passed on to the US government. Recent sources have clearly stated that the second incident did not happen, but the US government was not told that the second incident did not happen in 1964.

Nowadays, it is also disputed whether the first incident even happened. Some historians believe the Gulf of Tonkin incident did happen but not in the way it was described. The incident that occurred was possibly just a result of "friendly fire."[xxiii]

Regardless of what actually happened, the US retaliated and, under orders from President Lyndon B. Johnson, began to send more troops to fight on behalf of the Republic of Vietnam. Since the US supported the democratic South and the Soviet Union supported the communist North, the superpowers were yet again involved in another proxy war.

Combat in Vietnam

WWI was mainly fought in trenches. WWII is known for the bombing raids that took place, but the war in Vietnam was a different kind of war. It was a war in which the enemy was hidden.

The Americans were fighting with the South Vietnamese army. The North Vietnamese army also had people on its side: the Viet Cong. The Viet Cong were based in the South too.

This means the Americans and the Republic of Vietnam were fighting against an army that existed across the entire country. This made the war difficult and complicated. It was hard for the US Army to work out who was truly their enemy. The North Vietnamese members would often attack and then disappear underground. They used the environment to hide after attacking, often hiding in the jungles. To find their opposition, the Americans used a number of ways.

To overcome their hidden enemy, the Americans used chemicals. A chemical that the US Army used, one that people have often heard about, was Agent Orange. The chemical was used to destroy the terrain the Viet Cong hid in. The US government knew the chemicals would be dangerous for the people that were in the environment, but it realized it was a great way to uncover the enemy. Just like in the wars before, the US Army bombed cities they thought the Viet Cong were hiding in. However, the Americans couldn't really be sure who was a civilian and who was a member of the Viet Cong. This meant many citizens were killed and, in some instances, entire villages were massacred in an effort to win the war. The war affected the civilians in ways that can still be felt in Vietnam even to this day.

Discontent for the war grew in America, and protests sprung up across the country. Protests began to develop nationally in 1965, and the movement to end the war became huge by the end of the decade. It originated with students in the United States who decided they needed to do something in order for the war to end. As the protests grew, the people pressured the government to begin to withdraw troops from Vietnam. War without public support is hard to maintain.

An image of a woman holding out a flower to military police during an anti-war protest
https://en.wikipedia.org/wiki/File:Vietnamdem.jpg

The Tet Offensive

The discontent for the Vietnam War grew even more after the Tet Offensive. This happened in 1968. The Viet Minh and the Viet Cong had planned attacks in South Vietnam. The attacks happened during a time called Tet, which is the New Year's holiday in Vietnam.

The aim was to simultaneously attack cities in South Vietnam. It was not as effective as planned. The North Vietnamese army did not debilitate the US and South Vietnamese forces to the extent they wanted. The city of Saigon, which they captured as a result of the attack, was not held for too long.

Regardless, the Tet Offensive opened the eyes of many of the American public. Like the French population when their army was in Vietnam, much of the US population that still supported the war now began to question American involvement in Vietnam. The people realized many of the Vietnamese did not want the US to be in their country. The televised news reports made this even clearer. The American population that had previously found themselves far from the horrors of war during WWI and WWII and beyond finally had a war from which they could no longer escape. It was right in front of their eyes, as this was the first major broadcasted war. The American public, who originally thought the war was being fought for the greater good and that North Vietnam was incapable of such an ambitious assault, saw the reality of war.

Furthermore, the African Americans, who had been fighting for civil rights during the war, protested against it too because it affected African American communities on another level. African American soldiers were sent to fight in areas in Vietnam where it was clear they were just being sent to die. Even though they had the US flag on their uniforms, they were not fighting in the same way as their counterparts who had lighter skin.

Historians report the Tet Offensive was the event that made the US government believe they could not win the war. However, according to many of the people that currently live in Vietnam, the war was lost before it started.[xxiv] The Vietnamese people wanted freedom. They had lived under French rule and wanted to govern their own country. The United States winning the war would not have given them the freedom they wanted. Many Vietnamese people fought on the side of communism because it was a route for their country to gain freedom. During the war, Vietnamese citizens would allow Viet Cong meetings to take place in their homes, and many supported the Viet Minh because it stood for Vietnamese independence.

Drawing to an End

Just before the 1970s arrived, the US had been slowly withdrawing its troops, leaving the Southern army with less support.

In 1974, the Paris Peace Accords was signed. Although fighting by both sides continued after this, it was an important treaty because it allowed the war to come closer to its end. The US promised to reduce the military support it gave to the Republic of Vietnam. The Republic of Vietnam did not think support from the US would completely stop, but this was later seen to be untrue.

The army in the North decided to see how far the treaty would go in terms of US involvement. Their original leader, Ho Chi Minh, had died four years before, but that did not stop them from trying to achieve their original goal. They attacked South Vietnam in November 1974. As they hoped, the US did not get involved. The Viet Minh and Viet Cong decided to continue and attacked Saigon. Saigon was captured as a result. This event was the end of the war, and since then, unlike North and South Korea, the country has been reunited under one leader. As of this writing, Vietnam remains a communist country.

The US originally decided to get involved in the Vietnam War because it had promised to fight against communism. Vietnam was devastated due to the effect the war had on the nation. Chemicals used by the Americans left the Vietnamese people and also American veterans with fatal burns and birth defects. Vegetation was destroyed due to chemical warfare, not to mention the masses of bombs dropped on the nation.

After WWII, the public view of war changed in Europe and the United States. Furthermore, fewer people saw colonization in a positive light. Americans finally saw the truth of what war was truly like, which helped them to reach their own conclusion about whether they thought the war in Vietnam was positive or not. This led to mass protests in America. The lack of support the government received from the population and the backlash after the Tet Offensive helped it to see that this war would be unwinnable.

Chapter 6 – From Kennedy to Carter: The Internal Changes

The 1960s started intensely. John F. Kennedy (JFK) had not been president for long before multiple events occurred. He managed the failed Bay of Pigs incident in Cuba in 1961. The infamous Berlin Wall was built that same year too. Just to make matters more intense, the Cuban Missile Crisis happened the year after. It was tense abroad but also at home for several reasons. The 1950s saw Black Americans fighting for their civil rights. This exploded in the 1960s, a decade that saw many groups of people fighting for their rights and for change in their country.

The Civil Rights Movement

Black Americans had been fighting for their civil rights since slavery had been abolished. Huge sparks of the civil rights movement began in the decade before the 1960s. Black Americans had staged many protests to fight against the constant discrimination they faced, as the racial problem America had on its hands kept being pushed to the side. Some would argue that even in the 21st century, the United States still has not fully dealt with the problem of racism.

This sign was put up across the street from a federal housing project in Detroit, Michigan
https://en.wikipedia.org/wiki/File:We_want_white_tenants.jpg.

In 1955, Black Americans staged the Montgomery bus boycott to protest segregation on public buses. Although Rosa Parks was not the first Black American to refuse to move to the designated seats for Blacks at the back of the bus, her actions in 1955 sparked a major movement. Protests like these grew and became commonplace. They continued into the next decade, with sit-ins becoming more popular. Sit-ins took place to bring awareness to things like unfair hiring practices and to desegregate public spaces, such as lunch counters.

The media played a part in the success of the civil rights movement, showing the evidence of the Emmett Till murder. Emmett Till was a fourteen-year boy who was kidnapped, tortured, and then lynched in 1955, before the Montgomery bus boycott. An all-white jury found the men responsible for the murder not guilty; a year later, the men confessed to the crime, although they received no punishment from the law for their wrongdoing. The media televised and reported on the protests that occurred afterward, which helped the civil rights activists push for change.[xxv]

When the protestors were attacked by the police, such as in the well-known attack that happened in Birmingham, Alabama, in 1963, the images were seen internationally. This was the same protest that saw prominent civil rights leader Martin Luther King Jr. arrested; he would be arrested nearly thirty times throughout his life. The protests put pressure on the government and, in particular, Kennedy, who was still president at the time.

Kennedy was a firm believer in civil rights legislation. However, he had a hard time getting the Senate to agree with him. Although JFK started the process of passing the Civil Rights Act, he died before it could become law. He was assassinated in 1963 in Dallas, an event that shook the United States (if you ask people who were alive then, they most likely will be able to tell you what they were doing when they heard the news). Once he died, Lyndon B. Johnson (LBJ) became the next president of America.

Johnson was Kennedy's vice president, and he finished the work Kennedy had started, ensuring the civil rights bill was passed. The Civil Rights Act of 1964 outlawed discrimination based on race, color, religion, sex, and national origin. Schools and public places could no longer be segregated. In essence, it was passed to make sure that all citizens were granted equal protection under the law.

LBJ was a president who, like Kennedy, wanted to elevate society; this included people from all backgrounds. LBJ's policy known as the Great Society was aimed at fighting against poverty through programs that helped more people go to university. The programs helped citizens gain employment and for the poor and the older generation to get adequate medical care. Although government funds helped to ensure poverty was reduced, plans to continue in an upward direction were halted. This is because, at the time, American forces were still fighting in Vietnam, and funding was needed to continue the war effort.

Another prominent death occurred in the 1960s. Malcolm X was assassinated less than two years after Kennedy. Malcolm was a prominent activist who often spoke about the economic and political changes that should happen in order for civil rights to be achieved. He fought for change during the 1950s and 1960s. Malcolm X fought for change in the police system by fighting against police brutality. He taught about self-love instead of falling under the pressures that Black Americans faced in the 1960s. He did not want Black Americans to conform to American society since they did not have an equal voice. Malcolm X is often seen as a controversial figure, with many people contrasting his methods to Martin Luther King Jr. Regardless of how one feels about his tactics, Malcolm X helped bring attention to the civil rights movement, and he is seen positively by many in the Black community today.

An image of MLK and Malcolm X
This image is available from the United States Library of Congress's Prints and Photographs division under the digital ID cph.3d01847;
https://en.wikipedia.org/wiki/File:MLK_and_Malcolm_X_USNWR_cropped.jpg

Alongside the fight for civil rights, the war that had been brewing in Vietnam had resumed. President Johnson decided it was the right decision to send more troops to Vietnam to fight against the communist North and the Viet Cong in 1965. This sparked protests. Many students who had been protesting for civil rights for Black

Americans also decided to use their passion to protest against the Vietnam War.

1968: The Year of Protests

Protesting for rights took more than one shape and form in the 1960s. By 1968, there were many groups that fought for their rights.

The Vietnam War protest grew. One of the reasons for this was the fact the public was able to see live television reports from Vietnam. In 1968, the Tet Offensive happened, with the North Vietnamese army attacking areas in the South. When the public saw the reality of war, anti-war protests began to evolve and grow.

Music and literature helped other groups to fight for their rights. Prominent singers like Marvin Gaye and Bob Dylan released tracks that protested the war and fueled the public's passion for protesting against it.

Speaking of music, a counterculture arose during the 1960s, with many of the youths involved being referred to as hippies. Hippies often used drugs, like LSD and weed, and embraced unique fashion trends and ideas, like living in communes. They were known for listening to psychedelic rock, but the 1960s were influential in other ways in regard to music. The British Invasion, which saw bands like the Beatles and the Rolling Stones, was huge in the US. Motown music was massive as well, bringing the Supremes, the Four Tops, and Aretha Franklin to the top of the charts. Pop and rock were being reinvented, with surf rock and bubble gum pop being just some of the many different genres to come to the forefront. The famous Woodstock Festival in New York celebrated the ideas of love and peace, ideas that hippies fervently believed, while featuring major artists of the time like Janis Joplin and Jimi Hendrix.

An image of the stage at Woodstock. You might notice the muddy ground; it rained heavily during the concert

Hippies also believed in the sexual revolution. In the United States, women had been continuing to fight for their rights. In the 1960s, the women's movement caught a second wave.[xxvi] The feminist movement sprouted due to a number of factors. Many women were reading feminist literature, such as *The Feminine Mystique*, which helped to show that women were not satisfied with raising kids and taking care of the household; they wanted more in life. Another factor was that legislation showed that women were not equal to men. One example of this is that it was legal for companies to fire a woman who had become pregnant. Additionally, women also received, on average, 40 percent less than men for carrying out the same job as them. Numerous states still prohibited women jurors. All of this and more fueled women to fight for equality.

Many females were unsatisfied with knowing that they were judged negatively for having sexual intercourse before marriage, yet it was seen as normal for men to do so. Many women were tired of this and wanted to be free from this double standard that society had set for them. In the early 1960s, women were seen as beings who had sex to procreate; however, as the women's movement developed, so did the sexual revolution. The women's movement aimed to change the way society saw women and to show society that they had sexual desires too.[xxvii]

The sexual revolution, which impacted both men and women, went deeper than this, though. Yes, sex was beginning to be viewed differently in terms of monogamy, but other things began to be normalized as well. The pill (which was first approved in 1960), pornography, and masturbation are just some of the things that began to be accepted more and more as the years passed. In the 1970s, President Richard Nixon began sending federal funds to Planned Parenthood, and the Supreme Court legalized abortion through *Roe v. Wade.* The LGBTQ movement, which is separate from the sexual revolution, began in earnest in the late 1960s, with the LGBTQ community encouraging people to take a harsher stand against hatred and to be proud of who they were. Although some still might view these things as controversial today, they allowed for a different kind of expression, one that is still evolving.

Other Events of the Late 1960s

Due to the racial inequality in America, protests continued after the Civil Rights Act was passed in 1964. The law, along with the Voting Rights Act of 1965, went in the right direction, but the laws had not done enough to establish equality. One example of that is the continual issue of police brutality that the Black community faced.

The Black Panthers, a group that was established in 1966, looked for a different approach than Martin Luther King Jr. After numerous incidents of police brutality, they decided to form a group to seek out civil rights for themselves. They offered communities protection through the use of weapons and did work in the community to help educate children. Although this organization is often seen as controversial, scholars today believe the Black Panthers were one of the most influential Black movements in the 1960s.

On April 4th, 1968, Martin Luther King Jr., who had been fighting for civil rights for Black Americans, was assassinated. Since the 1950s, MLK had been leading protests in order to bring attention to the injustices Black Americans faced. Although he is most often remembered for his "I Have a Dream" speech, Martin Luther King had more layers to his political career. He campaigned for the poorest demographics to get help from the government, and he was against the war in Vietnam. As a result of his death, riots broke out across America. The United States had seen riots over the years, but the riots after MLK died were severe, oftentimes ending with the National Guard being deployed.[xxviii]

Ushering in a New President

Along with the 1960s being the decade of protests, it was also the decade of assassinations. In 1968, Robert (Bobby) Kennedy had been campaigning to become the Democratic candidate for the presidential election that year. In line with some of LBJ's liberal policies and the fight for equality from numerous groups, Kennedy fought for equality for Black Americans, Native Americans, and the poor. Furthermore, he had political experience. He had been working in politics for years, and he had worked as the attorney general when his brother, JFK, was the president of the US. Another reason for his popularity was the war in Vietnam. While campaigning, Robert focused his campaign message on the fact that he wanted the US military to withdraw from Vietnam. Despite his popularity, his chance to get elected did not come to pass, as he was assassinated months after MLK. He was shot on March 5th, 1968, and died a day later. Many agree that he likely would have been elected had he lived.

However, the 1968 election still loomed, and in the end, the Republican candidate, Richard Nixon, was elected. Nixon's time as president could be best described as rocky. He was still president in 1973, which saw the first but not the only oil crisis of the decade. There was a shortage of oil since the Organization of Petroleum Exporting Countries (OPEC) had stopped imports of oil to the US.

The embargo lasted until March the next year and had an effect on other industries as well. Additionally, inflation had been occurring in America since the mid-1960s; however, the oil crisis worsened it.[xxix] Nixon had already tried to fix the problem of inflation by changing the way the dollar was valued by stopping the link between gold and the US dollar. However, this did not solve the problem of inflation; instead, it was exacerbated. When Nixon stepped down in 1974, President Gerald Ford, who was Nixon's vice president, tried to lessen the impact of inflation on the economy, but his efforts did little.

The problem with the economy can be described by the word stagflation. This means as inflation was rising, unemployment was low. President James (better known as Jimmy) Carter was elected in 1976, and his policy changes and the actions of Paul Volcker started to move the economy in the right direction. Volcker became the chairman of the Board of Governors and worked heavily on stabilizing the economy. In 1978, Carter declared the government had "reduced the unemployment rate by about 25 percent" and would continue to reduce government spending, helping the economy to move into recovery mode.[xxx] Although the economy did not stabilize until the 1980s, Carter's and Volcker's work played a large role in the economy's recovery.

Watergate

Before we move too far into the 1970s, we have to address the event that Nixon will always be best remembered for: the Watergate scandal. In May 1972, burglars broke into a building. However, it was not just any old building. It was the building the Democrats had been using as their headquarters. No one seemed to notice this had happened. However, criminals tend to return to the scene of the crime, and on June 17th, 1972, they did. And this time, the burglars were caught.

Investigators would later find out that the burglars had broken in the first time to locate information about the Democrats. The second break-in happened because the burglars had originally tried to plant bugs to listen to conversations, but they were not working properly. The burglars aimed to gain key information about the Democrats and their efforts in the election campaign.

After the investigation, two reporters, Bob Woodward and Carl Bernstein, discovered more than they thought possible. Despite the fact that the break-in did not resemble anything untoward, the reporters were encouraged by an informant to continue their investigation. The informant went by the name of Deep Throat, and he was a key player in uncovering the aim of the burglary. This informant was actually the associate director of the FBI at the time, Mark Felt.

A plan from Nixon and his team was created to stop the FBI from investigating the break-in. It worked. However, continuous investigations from the original newspaper reporters made it clear that the burglars were attached to the president. They even uncovered a large payment of $25,000 that linked the burglars and the president together. Nixon denied any involvement in knowing about or being involved in a crime like this. But this was just the beginning of the story.

Even to this day, it has been debated whether Nixon knew about this specific break-in; however, one thing that has not been debated is the fact that after the event was made public, Nixon tried to cover up the fact that his team of employees was involved.

The public believed Richard Nixon at this time, and he won the next election in 1972. The next year, on January 8th, the Watergate trial began. The burglars were on trial for their involvement in the break-in, and they all pled guilty.

During this time, the media had been sharing information about the investigation, including live broadcasts. In 1971, Nixon had installed video-recording equipment in the White House. This came to light during the trial. When this information became public, Nixon spent approximately three months keeping hold of the tapes. He knew they would reveal his involvement in the cover-up.

When the transcripts of the tapes were made public, it was clear that, as some had suspected, Nixon was involved in covering up his and his party's involvement in the Watergate break-in. This resulted in Nixon resigning on August 9th, 1974, the only US president to resign so far. Nixon was never actually impeached, although the process had already started in the House of Representatives. It was a smart move on Nixon's part; the trial likely would not have gone well for him, and by resigning, President Gerald Ford (Nixon's vice president) was able to pardon Nixon for any crimes.

But once this happened, the general public had another reason to see the government differently. This had already begun due to their loss of faith in the government due to the US involvement in the Vietnam War. Now, the public had a similar feeling about the government on a national level.

The 1960s and the 1970s were decades of change. The massive level of protests and legislative changes meant that by 1980, the US would never look the same again. The Watergate scandal was another event that changed America, leaving the public wondering how much they could trust the government and politicians in general. Furthermore, the 1960s was a decade that saw four prominent assassinations of leaders who were fighting for change in America. The leaders and the work they did is still remembered today.

Chapter 7 – The Cold War Phase II: From the Détente to the End

Toward the late 1960s, both of the superpowers, the Soviet Union and the United States, had their fair share of tense moments. The Cuban Missile Crisis of 1962 had proven just how real a nuclear war could be. By 1963, a hotline was set up between the Kremlin and the White House, ensuring direct communication between the two in case of another stand-off. The nuclear arms race had cost both the Soviets and the United States trillions of dollars and amounted to a massive amount of accumulated weaponry that would assure mutual destruction if either side pressed the button.

Though the Cuban Missile Crisis marked the end of the direct, head-butting conflict between the two superpowers for a while, across the world, ripple effects of the Cold War continued through proxy wars and confrontations.

In Southeast Asia, the US was suffering from the consequences of its entry into a struggle in Vietnam. With each US president, from Dwight D. Eisenhower to Lyndon B. Johnson, US involvement in Vietnam increased to the point of a full-on confrontation with massive casualties. The war expenses were huge, and America's involvement in the war weakened the trust many US citizens had in their government.

Tensions in the Middle East

In the Middle East, tensions between Israel and its neighbors, namely Syria, Jordan, and Egypt, had reached a fever pitch, resulting in a six-day war in 1967. With the United States advocating for Israeli democracy and Egypt relying on China and the Soviet Union for intelligence, the two superpowers were tested once again. Meanwhile, the Soviet Union was dealing with some internal issues of its own.

The Cold War in Europe

Things continued to escalate for the Soviets after the ousting of Nikita Khrushchev in 1964. His protégé, a new and more radical leader named Leonid Brezhnev, replaced him.

Though he had supported a more lenient system of rule, the moment Brezhnev stepped into power, he secured his grip. He eventually declared the Brezhnev Doctrine, which was his version of the Truman Doctrine. The Brezhnev Doctrine would be used to oppress any opposition to Moscow's rule within the Soviet Union, like the crushing of the 1968 liberation movement in communist Czechoslovakia. Brezhnev's doctrine would eventually justify invasions beyond the USSR's borders, putting an end to the period of softer relations between the US and the Soviet Union known as the détente or "release from tension." But as the 1970s rolled in, everybody was tired.

Tensions Cooling?

With both sides dealing with the effects of a frustrated population, it was time for a change, and the United States' thirty-seventh president took up that mantle. Richard Nixon entered office and sought to soften ties between the United States and communist nations.

In a radical and surprising move, Nixon pressed the United Nations to recognize the communist People's Republic of China and announced his intentions to visit the country. The move stunned many, as Nixon was a staunch anti-communist who had criticized President Truman's handling of the red scare and communism in America, stating that the administration "refused time and again to do anything about it."[xxxi] By 1967, however, he had softened his tune after the Vietnam War. President Nixon and First Lady Pat Nixon arrived in Beijing on February 21st, 1972, kicking off a new era of international relations. As the first sitting American president to visit mainland China, Nixon's week-long trip was heavily documented. It also further pushed the nation to seek an exit from the Vietnam War, as Americans saw the possibility of diplomatic relations between a capitalist and a communist state.

The trip also set the stage for another pivotal moment in history months later in May. With the arms race draining economic resources for both superpowers, the Moscow Summit resulted in a series of agreements, including the Strategic Arms Limitation Treaty (SALT). This was signed by Brezhnev and Nixon. The treaty limited the amount of anti-ballistic missiles each superpower could have and limited the manufacturing of strategic weapons for five years.

Brezhnev visited the United States in 1973 to sign an anti-nuclear war treaty. However, despite the open cooperation between the two powers, the proxy wars tied to them manifested yet again. Conflicts in the Middle East between Israel, Egypt, and Syria had opened old wounds. Not satisfied with the Israelis' victory in the Six-Day War and the land they conquered, Egypt and Syria launched an attack to reclaim the territory.

Tensions Heat Up Again

Again, the Soviets supplied the Arab countries with weapons, and the US supplied Israel. This proved to be a costly move for the United States, as the Organization of Petroleum Exporting Countries (OPEC) slapped an oil embargo on the US. This crippled the transport industry severely. By the time Washington and Moscow forced a treaty, the damage had been done, and Nixon's détente policy would struggle to get back on track.

The resignation of President Richard Nixon in 1974 left an unstable relationship with the Soviet Union, which crumbled a few years later. At that time, the Soviet Union aided in the spread of communism in newly liberated African countries, including Guinea, Mozambique, Ethiopia, and Angola. The US responded by backing guerrilla warfare groups that opposed communist leaders in these nations. This led to a messy and bloody series of civil wars across the continent. By 1978, the détente policy was hanging by a thread. It needed a successful show of cooperation. Enter the Camp David Accords, which were facilitated by US President Jimmy Carter.

Egypt, which was under the leadership of President Anwar Sadat, abandoned its Soviet allegiance because it wanted stronger ties with the US, as well as the return of the Sinai Peninsula, which had been captured in October 1973 during the Yom Kippur War. Israeli Prime Minister Menachem Begin was willing to listen, so the three engaged in what became the Framework for Peace in the Middle East.

The framework agreements were signed on September 17th, 1978, and they were meant to develop a strategy for the establishment of a Palestinian state, as well as the recognition of Israel as a sovereign nation by its Arab neighbors. It was a brief moment of calm, but by the same time next year, a major crack in US-Soviet relations would usher in a new Cold War era that would last until the fall of the Soviet Union.

In 1979, the US and the Soviet Union's interests in the oil- and gas-rich nation of Iran went head-to-head. The US backed the leader called Mohammad Reza Pahlavi, who was simply known as the Shah. He ruled from 1941 up until his ousting in 1979 during the Iranian Revolution. Those tired of the Shah's secular and repressive tactics and ruling style saw the US support of him as interfering in Iranian affairs. That tension mounted on November 4th, 1979, when Iranian militants broke into the US Embassy in Tehran, holding over 60 US citizens hostage for 444 days.

While President Carter dealt with negotiations for the lives of the US citizens, Leonid Brezhnev invaded Afghanistan. He justified this act with his Brezhnev Doctrine. Under the guise of maintaining the Afghan-Soviet Friendship Treaty, which had been set up in 1978, Brezhnev invaded Afghanistan to maintain the communist leadership that was wildly unpopular with the Afghan citizens. After the Communist Party leader was killed, Moscow sought to form a government that suited its ideals better. The US and Europe also collaborated to install Pershing II cruise missiles and rockets in Europe in response to the Soviets' deployment of Soviet SS-20s.

The deployment of US missiles led to a breakdown in Geneva talks and kicked up the arms race again. The détente was officially over, and the Cold War was back in effect. The United States retaliated further by funding the Mujahedeen, an Afghan rebel group that opposed the interference of the secular Soviet Union in what they deemed an Islamic affair. Additionally, the US boycotted the 1980 Moscow Olympics and further sanctioned the Soviet Union.

Support for the Afghan fundamentalist group increased when Ronald Reagan won the 1981 presidential election on an anti-détente campaign. Reagan's "peace through strength" initiatives led to the Regan Doctrine, which sought to defend democratic nations that needed help.

Reagan supported and heavily funded guerrilla fighters and rebels from several nations that the US saw as being under the threat of communist influence. The Soviet Union suffered another blow when long-time leader Leonid Brezhnev died in 1982. Two elderly leaders of the Soviet Union would die in rapid succession after Brezhnev, which weakened the Soviet Union's image of strength and leadership.

Reagan pressured the Soviet Union further by introducing the Strategic Defense Initiative. This was a space-based shield that would be able to deter and destroy nuclear missiles. It never came to pass, but the magnitude of the initiative threw the Soviet Union into rapidly developing more arms. This required the diversion of funds, which were originally used to run its satellite states, and threw the bloc into a downward economic spiral. On top of that, the Soviets were dealing with a costly war in Afghanistan. The war lasted nine years and stretched the bloc's military capabilities thin. Throughout the years, Reagan would increase his anti-communist campaigns.

Under his doctrine, Reagan invaded Grenada and overthrew the new government that was largely influenced by Marxist ideas in favor of a more Western-leaning leadership. While the Soviets were dealing with finding a new leader, Reagan expanded his controversial foreign policy. In 1986, a German nightclub often frequented by American servicemen was bombed by Libyan agents. As a result, Reagan ordered the bombing of key sites in Tripoli and Benghazi. A longstanding ally of the US, Britain, aided with the attack. It soured US-Libyan relations for years, with leader Muammar Gaddafi calling Reagan "mad" and "foolish."[xxxii]

The End of the Cold War

By 1985, Soviet Union leader Mikhail Gorbachev had inherited a nation that was crumbling. Trying to keep up with the arms race affected the Soviet Union economically. The low standard of living, which was brought about by an economic collapse, made citizens look toward independence. Preoccupied with building a new economically and socially strong republic, Gorbachev focused on national policy.

In the US, Reagan, often assisted by the CIA, continued carrying out anti-communist campaigns in Nicaragua. Nicaragua was already led by a socialist, Cuban-backed political party known as the Sandinistas. Reagan decided he needed a way to destabilize this, and he funded a rebel group known as the Contras.

To do this, Reagan and the CIA bypassed strict Congress rules on interference in Nicaragua. He and the CIA negotiated weapons deals with Iran, which was considered a US enemy after the hostage crisis. In addition, there had been another kidnapping of US citizens in

Lebanon by Iranian terrorists. This US group sold the Iranians weapons and used some of the proceeds to fund the Contras in Nicaragua. This was apparently done to obtain goodwill with moderate Iranians, but due to the clandestine nature of the operation, it was (and still is) easy for the public to think otherwise. When the information that over 1,500 missiles had been sold to Iran in November 1986, Reagan was criticized for "negotiating with terrorists" and funding conflicts abroad illegally.

In 1987, the end of the Cold War was near. The Soviet Union and the US signed the Intermediate-Range Nuclear Forces (INF) Treaty. This treaty outlined that both parties had to destroy all of their nuclear and conventional ground-launched ballistic and cruise missiles that fell within the 500- to 5,500-kilometer range.[xxiii] Gorbachev and Reagan signed it, signaling the beginning of the end of the Cold War.

Unlike previous Soviet leaders, Gorbachev shared a somewhat friendly relationship with the US, easing tensions. The conclusion to the Cold War lay in Gorbachev's two-part policy known as perestroika and glasnost. Glasnost focused on loosened political expressions, while perestroika targeted rebuilding the economy. Gorbachev also swept away Stalinist traditions by reintroducing the works of Russian writers like Boris Pasternak.

Gorbachev greatly reduced the influence of the secret police, also known as the KGB. He also introduced the idea of a multi-party election process, ushering democracy into the bloc. Gorbachev's economic policies followed open communist-capitalist integration, similar to China. This was mostly to strengthen the weak economy. The loosened political system meant satellite states could voice dissatisfaction without facing intense retaliation from Moscow. This led to the 1989 workers' revolution in Poland, and soon after that, the Berlin Wall fell.

It was clear that West Germany was prosperous while the quality of life in the East was low. Residents demanded free movement between East and West Berlin. Gorbachev facilitated the reunification of

Germany and did not oppose their entry into NATO either. By then, the US had transitioned from Reagan to George H. W. Bush, who took a soft approach toward the Soviet Union, sensing how fragile it had become.

After the Berlin Wall came down, the leaders in Moscow did not do much to reverse it. The Soviet Union was presumed dead. In 1991, the Baltic and Caucasus states erupted in protests, with Latvia and Lithuania demanding independence. Belarus and Ukraine soon declared their independence. Democratic candidate Boris Yeltsin replaced Gorbachev, who had resigned. After this, Yeltsin met with leaders from Belarus and Ukraine, forming the Commonwealth of Independent States (CIS) and formally dissolving the Soviet Union on December 25th, 1991.

By the beginning of the 1990s, the Cold War was officially over. The Berlin Wall had come down, and the Soviet Union had started to fall apart. The treaties signed between the US and the Soviet Union helped bring about the end of the Cold War, leaving the US to focus on other enemies. The enemies formed during the Cold War and the effects of the proxy wars that happened as a result of the waring superpowers can still be seen decades later.

Chapter 8 – Reagan and Bush: New Right and New Order

On a domestic scale, the beginning of the 1980s started harshly. The American population had dealt with two oil crises in the previous decade. Furthermore, they had been dealing with high unemployment and an economy. Although former President Jimmy Carter and Volcker had begun to fix the economic issues, there was still much to do.

When the former actor Ronald Reagan became president in January 1981, he promised to do things very differently. Reagan had won the 1980 presidential election by a landslide, beating President Jimmy Carter by 489 to 49 electoral college votes.[xxxiv] Reagan put solving the economic problems at the center of his campaign.

Changes in American Society

Reagan was part of a new generation of Republican politicians seen as the "New Right." Unlike other right-wing politicians in the 1960s and 1970s, who had increasingly made peace with the size of the state, Reagan and his New Right supporters believed that the government's size was holding ordinary Americans back. They were uneasy with the federal tax rate and expensive government programs, such as

Medicare and Medicaid. Also, they were uncomfortable with the changing social fabric of America.

Since the Vietnam War, the country had become increasingly liberal; more civil rights were granted to women and people from various backgrounds. However, the New Right believed that the ongoing social changes needed to be halted.

President Reagan attempted to bring America back to a more socially conservative time. He tried to reverse the effects of the 1973 ROE V. WADE ruling on abortion by withdrawing federal funds to non-governmental agencies that engaged in abortion consultations.[xxxv] When Nixon was in power, he waged the "War on Drugs" to better American society. This war was ramped up further when Reagan entered office. Meanwhile, a push was made to convince drug users of the error of their ways. In part, this took the form of the famous "Just Say No" campaign, which was spearheaded by First Lady Nancy Reagan.[xxxvi]

American society was slowly changing in other ways too. The Rust Belt states lost much of their traditional industry, and a population drift began since industrial cities lost citizens to places with better job prospects. The steel hub of the US, Pittsburgh, Pennsylvania, lost almost 136,000 people under the age of 35 between 1980 and 1990.[xxxvii]

Education also changed. Reagan legalized school prayer and attempted a federal ban on desegregated bussing.[xxxviii] President George H. W. Bush, on the other hand, was softer in tone when he took charge in 1989, promoting civic responsibility and volunteering through his "points of light" awards scheme.[xxxix]

Reagan and the Economy

In order to deal with the economic problems, Reagan, under a collection of policies dubbed "Reaganomics," sought to cut taxes, lower government spending, and deregulate large portions of the American economy. This began with the Economic Recovery Act of

1981, which passed one of the largest tax cuts in American history into law.[xl] Regan was influenced by the ideas of the economist Arthur Laffer and believed that if taxes were reduced, people and businesses would be able to spend and invest more, which would create more economic activity and generate more tax revenue as a result.[xli]

Reagan's plans were blown off track, though. In an attempt to calm inflation, the US Federal Reserve had raised interest rates. However, the result of the increased rate was to push down consumer and business spending. As a result, in 1981, America was plunged into its worst recession since the Great Depression.[xlii]

The Reagan Recession lasted into 1982 and resulted in the loss of over one million jobs. However, this did not last, and the economy rebounded sharply the following year with a growth rate of 4.6 percent. This increased to 7.2 percent in 1984.[xliii] That same year, Reagan was reelected as president once again by a landslide. Whether Reaganomics had a positive or negative effect on America is still debated. The tax cuts implemented by Reagan did not pay for themselves. Consequently, America's national debt ballooned by 186 percent during his time in office.[xliv]

Meanwhile, for many Americans, the effect of the tax cuts was canceled out by decreases in spending on government programs. The standard of living for single-income families fell during the 1980s, and adjusted for inflation, the average American earned less in 1989 than in 1983. But expectations of the government changed, and the effects would be felt beyond Reagan.

His successor, George Herbert Walker Bush, was popular with conservatives, especially as a result of his speech in 1988 when he asked the Republican National Convention to "read my lips, no new taxes."[xlv] Once elected, he went back on that very promise. The change was felt across the aisle too. In the 1960s, the Democrats had introduced many of the programs that Reagan rolled back, but when Bill Clinton came to the White House in 1993, he declared that the "era of big government is over."[xlvi] He would do little in his eight years in office to reverse many of the changes implemented by Reagan and Bush.

Neoconservatism

The rise of the New Right was accompanied and often complemented by the rise of another Right-wing ideology: Neoconservatism. It had sprouted in the 1960s in opposition to the increasingly liberal society that was forming in America. They shared many of the views held by the New Right, as they believed that America's economy was stagnating and that the nation had lost touch with its moral values. But the area in which Neoconservatives were perhaps most influential was foreign policy. They believed that America should not just seek to contain its enemies but also actively guide the world. If necessary, such guidance should take the form of military intervention.

Neoconservatives were increasingly found in positions of power on the American Right in the 1980s, and they found much to like about President Reagan. Just as he stepped away from the past's economic orthodoxies, Reagan also marked a crucial change in foreign policy. His collection of views became known as the Reagan Doctrine.

The Reagan Doctrine

Previous administrations had called for the Soviet Union and communism at large to be prevented from expanding. The Reagan Doctrine was more aggressive, and its aim was to eliminate communism altogether, branding the Soviet Union as "an evil empire."[xlvii] In practice, the doctrine meant supporting counter-revolutionary movements in communist countries. Reagan backed the Afghans, who were rebelling against the Soviet Union, and Angolans attempting to undermine their government.

In 1983, America sent over seven thousand troops to Grenada to crush a communist uprising. They also supported the Contra opposition to communism in Nicaragua. The latter led to one of the major scandals of the Reagan presidency: the 1986 Iran-Contra Affair.

The crisis occurred after America broke an arms embargo on Iran and sold the country weapons; it then diverted the proceeds toward the Contras in breach of national law. Events surrounding the Iran-Contra Affair hit Reagan's popularity seriously, but he insisted he did not know he had broken the law.[xlviii]

However, one thing is certain: Reagan's presidency coincided with the irreversible decline of the Soviet Union. For all of Reagan's rhetoric on defeating communism, he also pursued diplomatic channels to end the Cold War. He met the Soviet Premier Mikhail Gorbachev in Geneva in November 1985 and flew to Reykjavik, Iceland, for an unsuccessful nuclear disarmament summit in 1986. He would later appeal to the Soviet leader's sense of morality by asking him to "tear down" the Berlin Wall in a famous speech in 1987.[xlix] The end of the Cold War took place under Bush, but the beginning of the end took place under Reagan.

The Cold War Draws Close

With the Cold War reaching its conclusion, the world President H. W. Bush inherited in 1989 was very different from when Reagan came to office. Bush was less combative than his predecessor and took a more cautious approach to foreign affairs; he was unsure whether relations with the Soviets would remain close. Despite this, while he was president, a significant moment in history happened, as the Berlin Wall fell in 1989. This occurred amid a wave of anti-communist revolutions across Europe. The Soviet Union, meanwhile, went through a period of major liberalization before finally collapsing in 1991.

In 1990, Bush summed up the changes in a speech to a joint session of Congress. In it, he said that "A New World Order could now emerge."[l] He meant that the end of the Cold War presented the world with an opportunity to change its ways. Bush wanted more prominent countries to defend smaller ones from attack to preserve world peace. However, the speech was not just about the fall of communism because the president was also concerned about events in Iraq.

The Gulf War

After a dispute about oil siphoning, Iraqi dictator Saddam Hussein declared war on Kuwait on August 2nd, 1990. Within two days, Iraqi troops had conquered Kuwait and sought to occupy the country. On January 17th, 1991, an American-led coalition, which was backed by a UN resolution, invaded Iraq and overwhelmed its military. The conflict, which would become known as the Gulf War, ended on February 28th after the Bush administration declared a ceasefire. The Iraqi forces had been expelled from Kuwait.

In the short term, the perceived success of the conflict in the minds of the general public pushed President Bush's approval ratings up to the highest ever recorded at that point.[ii] As a result, he was strongly favored to win the 1992 presidential election. However, he lost, as his opponent, Democrat Bill Clinton, ran a successful campaign on the state of the economy. Nonetheless, Bush is regarded as a president whose strengths lay in foreign policy, and he found himself in office during perhaps the biggest period of change in global affairs since the end of the Second World War.

Conflicts in Europe

The end of the Cold War did not prevent conflict from returning to Europe in the early 1990s. The collapse of communism had created a power vacuum in some European nations, which led to a build-up of militant nationalists. The biggest example of this was the breakup of Yugoslavia.

The country had been a federation of Eastern European republicans run under a communist system. In 1991, everything changed when Slovenia decided to leave, followed by Croatia in the same year and then Bosnia and Herzegovina in 1992. War occurred in Croatia following its departure, and this was just the first of several conflicts that occurred in the former Yugoslavian republics.

In Bosnia, a division between Bosnian Serbs who wanted to remain part of modern-day Serbia and Bosnian Muslims who wanted independence resulted in a protracted and violent conflict. Numerous acts of ethnic cleansing occurred, which concerned the US government. In 1995, an American-backed peace agreement known as the Dayton Accords ended the conflicts by splitting Yugoslavia into smaller nations. But America would once again be drawn into the politics of the former Yugoslavia in 1998 when Kosovar separatist forces rebelled against the Serbian government.

A crackdown was launched, and violence ensued. NATO gave the Serbs an ultimatum to end the conflict, but they refused. Airstrikes were launched in March 1999, and eleven weeks later, they bowed to NATO's demands, allowing peacekeeping forces to enter the country. The Serbian president, Slobodan Milosevic, would later be tried for crimes against humanity for his actions in Bosnia, Croatia, and Kosovo.[lii]

The 1980s and early 1990s saw the division between the conservatives and the liberals solidified. The population showed the presidents in office that while foreign policy was important, domestic policy could not be forgotten. As the era concluded, it seemed as if many of the tensions of the 20th century would not be around in the 21st century. The world had changed dramatically, and the people had a new era to look forward to. This was sadly not to be the reality in which America and the global community found themselves, though.

Chapter 9 – The Challenges of the 1990s

The 1990s began with winds of change from behind Europe's Iron Curtain, bringing an air of optimism. The specter of the Cold War and communism that had hung over the US for so many years was finally fading. In the last months of 1989, communist regimes, whose grips on society had seemed unshakable, were now wavering. In Czechoslovakia and Poland, previously unthinkable transfers of power occurred peacefully, as both countries' communist parties lost control of their governments. In East Germany, the starkest symbol of the Cold War, the Berlin Wall, had fallen. By the end of 1991, the entire Soviet Union had crumbled.

The world was opening up again, and the United States stood as its unchallenged standard-bearer. The decade to follow shone with possibility: the American economy boomed, the internet grew from an oddity to a fixture in the majority of households, the American military dominated conflicts in smaller regions throughout the world, and globalization ran at full steam. Still, in the midst of this optimism lay seeds and hints of the challenges to come in the new millennium. This new age contained political controversies, the dangers of climate change, emotionally charged debates about the role of LGBTQ rights in society, and shocking terrorist attacks.

A Recession Leads to a Booming Economy

With the fall of the Soviet Union, Americans had reasons for optimism. The strength of the American economy had prevailed over the communist systems. The West's democratic and capitalist ideologies were still standing at the end of the Cold War. However, everything was not rosy, and the 1990s began with the American economy mired in a significant recession.

Several factors led to this recession, not the least of which was the shuttering of thousands of savings and loan institutions at the end of the previous decade. There was also an intense increase in energy costs due to conflict in the Middle East.

With savings and loan institutions closing at a rapid rate, Americans had fewer bank options through which to finance mortgages. The ripple effect continued as usual, and a decrease in mortgages led to significantly fewer new construction projects.

This was a painful time for this sector in the American economy, which is typically a huge producer of jobs. The timing could hardly have been worse, as the Gulf War in Iraq and Kuwait led to massive increases in energy prices due to the disruption of the oil market. The price of oil increased twofold over the course of the war.[liii] With fewer jobs available and higher energy prices, the recession led to no small amount of economic pain for the average American.

This pain was temporary. After 1991, the American economy rebounded and continued to steadily grow through the end of the decade, with increases of over 3 percent in gross domestic product (GDP) every year.[liv] Increased globalization and a boom in the technology sector often receive the credit for this growth.

With the Cold War concluded, the global market took off, and American companies did business all over the world. The signing of the North American Free Trade Agreement (NAFTA) demonstrated the new interdependence of countries in the global economy and eased trade restrictions between the United States, Canada, and Mexico.

Unemployment rates also plummeted. From 1992 until the end of the decade, the national unemployment rate went from 8 percent to approximately 4 percent. Additionally, the median income increased by 10 percent. The poverty rate fell by four points, and the stock market quadrupled in value.[lv]

As always, whenever there is a boom, it is not positive for everyone. Income inequality rose, and the gap between America's top 1 percent and the rest of the population continued to get wider. This trend continued into the 21st century.[lvi]

The Digital Revolution and the Rise of the Internet

The digital revolution helped drive this new global interconnectivity. Technology companies like IBM and General Electric had previously dominated the computer industry, and their expensive machines were primarily used in other corporations' business models. However, computers found a place in the American home in the 1990s. Companies like Microsoft and Apple had finally gained a significant foothold in a large number of American homes with personal computers (PCs). By 1999, over half the homes of Americans with some form of college education had their own personal computers.[lvii]

With computers now at many Americans' fingertips, greater possibilities for digital communication and commerce arose. The 1990s brought about the dawn of the internet as a tool for the general population, whereas previously, it had been a tool for the military. The World Wide Web was birthed in 1990, and computers in the US quickly connected to the internet.

Innovative American companies used the World Wide Web as an opportunity to make a profit. E-commerce, email, and e-banking all became buzzwords and changed how Americans did business.

Companies like Amazon, Yahoo, eBay, and Google, during the so-called dot-com bubble, were driven by the exciting new possibilities present on the web.

The growth of the internet challenged lawmakers' abilities to keep up with the changes. The landscape shifted quickly, with companies rising and falling on an open new frontier. Even in the 21st century, internet regulation has still been a topic of discussion for lawmakers.

The internet also presented another challenge for those in the public eye: the instantaneous spread of unflattering information. The internet changed how journalists broke stories, and the monopoly that major papers and TV channels had was drifting away. News on the internet nearly brought down the president of the United States in the 1990s.

The Clintons Define American Politics

One cannot tell the story of America in the 1990s without the Clintons. Their story involves the success of the American economy, their centrist approach to taxes, a conflicting record on LGBTQ issues, and, of course, the growing political polarization driven by his impeachment.

Most agree that Clinton's appeal to the country stemmed from his posturing as a practical centrist on many issues, including taxes and the size of the government. A Southern Democrat, he had achieved wild popularity as the governor of Arkansas, winning election to the office three times. That success gave him momentum to gain influence in the Democratic Party and earned him the presidential nomination in 1992. That same year, Clinton won the national election.

Due to his centrist stance, several pieces of legislation that passed were based on compromise. The "Don't Ask, Don't Tell" policy is a prime example. Clinton originally aimed to end discrimination against gay members of the military, but this led to controversy among many high-ranking generals and much of the American public. Don't Ask,

Don't Tell was a clear compromise. Instead of explicitly excluding LGBTQ Americans from participating in military service, which was previously the case, the new policy simply did not require military members to disclose their sexual preferences. As long as members of the LGBTQ community did not declare their sexuality, they were allowed in the military. Of course, this negatively impacted the LGBTQ community since they were forced to hide their sexuality.

The economy was strong during Clinton's presidency, but his presidency had failures. Clinton had hoped to create a system of universal healthcare. He placed First Lady Hilary Clinton in charge of a task force for healthcare reform. This was not popular among the conservatives in Congress, and various lobbyists in the medical industry made sure the program was unsuccessful. Clinton's pragmatism did achieve successful legislation in another area, though: gun law reform.

Clinton signed the Federal Assault Weapons Ban into law in 1994 as part of an effort to decrease violent crime. At that point, gun law reform was a huge topic of discussion in the US and has continued to be since then. Although loopholes still existed, the law did decrease access to many types of semi-automatic weapons, which was a long-desired outcome for Democrats.

Just as a discussion of the 1990s is incomplete without the Clintons, Clinton's presidency is incomplete without a discussion of his impeachment.

The details are widely known. Clinton had a sexual relationship with a White House intern named Monica Lewinsky and subsequently lied about it. In the scope of American history, it highlights two major trends and developments. The first development is the rise of internet journalism. After the Watergate building was broken into for the second time in June 1972, the story broke in a major newspaper. The Lewinsky scandal broke in a small, conservative blog online called the Drudge Report. The impeachment also highlighted the continual divide between the Democrats and

Republicans. Congress voted to acquit Clinton during the impeachment trial, but this happened entirely along party lines. In the Senate, not a single Democrat voted to impeach, and only five Republicans voted to acquit.

America Plays on the World's Stage

While America no longer faced any major military threats, that does not mean its military was inactive. America showed itself as a key player in several conflicts around the globe and in other diplomatic proceedings to address a massive security issue: climate change.

Firstly, the American military showed a willingness to play a role in global conflicts early on in the decade during the Gulf War. When Iraqi dictator Saddam Hussein invaded the much-smaller oil-rich Kuwait in 1990, President George H. W. Bush wasted no time in mobilizing US forces. Although Iraq's army was the world's fourth-largest at the time, the overwhelming air superiority and technological advantages of the US military were too much. Combat between the two nations lasted a little over a month.

A similar pattern followed in Yugoslavia when the ethnic cleansing of Albanians in Kosovo came to light. The US mobilized a coalition of NATO forces to carry out a strategic bombing campaign. The coalition's air force faced little resistance, and the conflict was over within three months, resulting in Yugoslav President Slobodan Milosevic's loss of power and eventual conviction for his war crimes.

The United States also played a role in international diplomacy on climate change, starting with the Rio Climate Summit of 1992 (officially known as the United Nations Conference on Environment and Development) and continuing with the Kyoto Protocol of 1997. As the world's largest economic power, America's role greatly affected the scope of these environmental agreements and their eventual ineffectiveness. American diplomats often complicated the negotiations due to conflicting goals on fossil fuel usage, and the US eventually failed to sign the Kyoto agreement.

The Threat of Terrorism Grows

Since the end of World War II, Americans had lived in a nuclear world. They lived in a world where their military and the military of their greatest adversary had access to weapons of frightening power, and those weapons constantly stood at the ready. With the end of the Cold War, the threat of nuclear war faded. In this decade after the fall of communism, a new threat began to emerge that would come to define the new millennium: terrorism, both foreign and domestic.

Often forgotten in the years since September 11th, 2001, is that the World Trade Center in New York City had first been attacked in the 1990s.

In 1993, terrorist Ramzi Ahmed Yousef, aided by followers of Sheikh Omar Abdel-Rahman, planned a bombing to topple the North Tower into the South Tower. They planted their giant homemade bomb in a van, left it in the underground parking garage, and sped off after lighting the fuses. The explosion killed six people but did not manage to destroy either tower. It did, however, leave thousands of people working in and visiting the towers emotionally shaken from the frantic evacuation—a scene that would play out again, far more tragically, only eight years later.

The World Trade Center bombing does not lay claim to the title of the most devastating terror attack of the 1990s. That distinction does not belong to Osama bin Laden, Al Qaeda, or any other foreign terrorist group. Instead, it belongs to Timothy McVeigh, a native-born, white American who previously served in the US Army. He carried out the devastating Oklahoma City bombing of 1995 in the hopes of inspiring a revolution against the government. He also utilized a homemade bomb planted in a van. McVeigh and accomplice Terry Nichols detonated a blast that destroyed a federal building, killing 168 people.[lviii]

The aftermath of the Oklahoma City bombing
https://en.wikipedia.org/wiki/File:Oklahomacitybombing-DF-ST-98-01356.jpg

The 1990s were a time of promise due to the rising use of computers and the internet. It allowed the world to become the global society it is today. President Clinton's time in the White House showed the American public how divided it had become politically. America had to deal with terrorist attacks during the decade; however, the domestic- and foreign-planned terror attacks, dreadful in their own right, were only preludes to what would come in the new millennium: a moment that shocked America and the world and the moment that unified millions of Americans in anguish and anger. It was a moment that set the course of American history for the next decades: September 11th, 2001.

Chapter 10 – Terror and Recession

Just a mere decade before the 2000s hit, the United States saw a development in technology that could have rivaled the Industrial Revolution. America also had to contend with the fact that its fight against terrorism was not only international but also domestic. America's first stint in Iraq in the early 1990s was deemed successful; however, the American military would be heading there again during this decade.

America in the 2000s is defined by a number of huge events: the 2000 election, the War on Terror, and Hurricane Katrina, just to name a few. These events left an impression on America and the world. Some of these impressions are still being experienced today.

Al Gore vs. George W. Bush

There have been a few contentious elections in America. The 2016 presidential election was one of them. Hillary Clinton lost the election but had more votes than Donald Trump; she lost due to the American voting system called the electoral college. The 2020 election could also be described as divisive. Trump strongly suggested the voting was rigged, which made the results sound questionable and ended up in an attack on the US Capitol. Although the 2000 election did not end in an insurrection, it also fits into a similar category as the above-mentioned elections.

The 2000 election pitted Republican George W. Bush against Democrat Al Gore. It was November 7th, 2000, and the votes for a close race between the candidates were being counted. In a mass of confusion, various television networks had declared one candidate the winner, while other networks declared in favor of the other. In the end, Bush was announced as the true victor, and Gore conceded. However, that was not the end of the story.

The election was close, and technically, both candidates had won but in different ways. Similar to the 2016 election, Gore had gained more votes, which meant he won the popular vote. However, that is not enough to become the president of the United States of America. Bush, on the other hand, won by gaining more votes through the system used in America called the electoral college.

The difficulty arose when it became clear that Al Gore had gained over 500,000 more votes than George W. Bush. After this revelation, Gore demanded a recount in the state of Florida. Florida was chosen because when the votes were counted, it was close. This typically results in a recount.

The process of recounting began. However, it is engulfed in controversy because the Florida secretary of state was tied to the Republican Party. Also, Bush's brother, Jeb, was the governor of Florida at the time. Now, this does not mean that they were involved in any wrongdoing. However, Florida's voters faced many problems, such as the sample ballot being different than the actual ballot, names being removed from the voter lists (approximately 15 percent were done so in error), and conflicting reports being issued on what to do with absentee ballots, among other things. Since the results were so close, these greatly impacted the final tally.

The recount occurred in four counties: Palm Beach, Volusia, Broward, and Miami Dade. By November 14th, the count was still going on, and a president had not yet been declared. This was, however, the recount deadline. The deadline was extended by the supreme court in Florida. Counties were then given until November 26th to finish the recount.

When November 26th had arrived, the recount was still not completed in all four counties, but the difference between the number of votes had lessened in gore's favor. The margin was 537 votes. Gore continued to fight the state of Florida to certify all the counties before declaring a winner.

However, the us supreme court decided it was time to bring this situation to a close. The decision for the US Supreme Court to take over will forever be debated. The one thing that stands true is that the undecided electoral vote had been dragged on, and after recounting the votes in Florida, it became clear that the voting process itself was not bulletproof. Originally, some of the voting cards had not been counted since it was unclear who the voter had actually voted for. This and the general inconsistency in the voting process is why the Supreme Court decided they needed to make a decision.

The Supreme Court decided that the voting count should stop, as Florida had violated the Eighteenth Amendment. This meant that Bush had officially won the election. The "real" winner of the 2000 election is still contested to this day. It was particularly unusual for the Supreme Court to get involved in an election. It is also argued that the decision to stop the recount was biased because there were more Republicans in the US Supreme Court at the time, and the decision went in the Republican's favor.

George W. Bush won the presidential election, but his two terms as president were not easy.

9/11

Arguably, September 11th, 2001, might have been one of the hardest trials George W. Bush experienced, and it is now and forever a "where were you on that day?" moment. Airplanes were hijacked and flown into the Twin Towers and the Pentagon. It was a day of tragedy. Once this had occurred, there was a desperate scramble to find the injured and dead within the rubble, as the buildings were crumbling and had caught on fire. Firefighters and civilians began to search for the lost and rescue the injured.

A fourth airplane was hijacked that day. However, in the eyes of the hijackers, it was unsuccessful. The civilians on the airplane prevented it from crashing into a building in Washington (likely the Capitol) by fighting against the hijackers. This resulted in the airplane crash-landing in Pennsylvania, killing everyone on board.

The September attacks resulted in many people injured, and just under three thousand people died.

An image of the South Tower after being struck by the plane
This file is licensed under the Creative Commons Attribution-Share Alike 2.0 Generic license; https://en.wikipedia.org/wiki/File:North_face_south_tower_after_plane_strike_9-11.jpg

On September 22nd, 2001, President George W. Bush addressed Congress. He discussed the attacks that had happened on September 11th, describing the "act of war" on American soil and the organization that had planned the attack: Al Qaeda.lix Bush made it clear that America would retaliate in different ways and called upon the "civilized" world to fight with him. It was then that the War on Terror truly began. This was a war that America and its allies fought against any organization that was based on an extreme form of Islam that threatened democracy.

Al Qaeda said they had planned the September attacks, and in retaliation, less than a month later, airstrikes began in Afghanistan to target Al Qaeda and another organization that worked in conjunction with them called the Taliban.

The US wanted to capture Osama bin Laden, who was Al Qaeda's leader at the time. Bin Laden was shot and killed by American forces around ten years after 9/11.

The airstrikes started on October 7th, 2001, and then moved on to a full-fledged war on October 19th. The war was not over as soon as many hoped; it ended up lasting twenty years.

From the American perspective, the initial part of the war was successful. The US and British armies, who were on the ground in Afghanistan, supported the Northern Alliance. The Northern Alliance was the organization that was strongly against the Taliban and Al Qaeda. The armies and their allies were able to force the Taliban and Al Qaeda out and hold a democratic election. Hamid Karzai was elected as the interim head of state in 2002.

However, the war did not stop there. It began to get worse between 2004 and 2007. American casualties, along with allies that had joined in the fight, had risen, and many of the public were hoping for troops to be withdrawn from Afghanistan. The continual war, which many thought would have been over by 2007, helped Barack Obama in his election campaign as the public's confidence in Bush and, by extension, the Republican Party had deteriorated.

An image of Barack Obama, the first African American US president.

https://en.wikipedia.org/wiki/File:Barack_Obama_addresses_joint_session_of_Congress_2009-02-24.jpg

The Iraq War

The War on Terror did not just stop with the retaliation of the September 11th attacks. America and its allies also declared war on Iraq. Saddam Hussein was the president of Iraq at the time. President Bush warned Saddam Hussein, stating that if he didn't leave the country, there would be military consequences.

Bush issued this warning because the American government believed that Saddam, alongside Al Qaeda, was also responsible for the September attack, believing they harbored Al Qaeda within the country. The US government and the British government were also convinced that Saddam Hussein had weapons of mass destruction (WMDs) and thought the war was the best way to gain these weapons so they couldn't be used against democratic nations. Bush and Tony Blair, who was the prime minister of the United Kingdom in 2001, made it clear that an attack on Iraq would lead to democracy being established in the nation.

When Saddam and his sons did not leave Iraq, American troops, with the backing of the UN, attacked Iraq approximately two years after the invasion of Afghanistan. On March 19th, 2003, the war in Iraq began.

Tanks and the military infiltrated the area, with casualties on both sides multiplying and buildings being destroyed. The US forces and their allies were able to capture Saddam on December 13th, and prior to that, they took control of the capital city of Baghdad. Like the invasion of Afghanistan, from a US perspective, the invasion had been a success, and it seemed it would continue this way. The capture of Saddam was televised, along with images of Iraqi citizens pulling down and destroying his statue. He would be killed in 2006 after being tried by an Iraqi tribunal.

But although Saddam had been captured, there was more work to be done. Troops stayed in Iraq, and the US tried to help to create a democratic government. While this was happening, violence surged in Iraq, and the US combated the problem by sending more troops, which helped to counteract the problem. However, the American public was continuously seeing soldiers return injured. They were aware that the US and its allies were fighting in two different wars in the Middle East.

Furthermore, terrorist attacks had shaken Europe, with one taking place in Madrid in 2004 and another in London the year after. Terrorism seemed to become a global thing.

By the time the UK and US troops had redrawn from Iraq, around 180,000 Iraqi civilians had died as a result of the conflict. However, some estimates go above 200,000. Saddam Hussein, who was often described as oppressive, was removed due to the invasion of Iraq. Another consequence of the war was the increase in extremism. After September 11th, war was declared on terrorism; however, wars need more than one side to be fought. Many extremist organizations gained momentum against the nation that declared war on them.

Hurricane Katrina

Hurricane Katrina was one of the biggest storms in the US in the decade and even in US history. On August 24th, 2005, a hurricane was building up in the Florida area, destroying homes. It continued to head toward Louisiana and the surrounding areas. Four days after the hurricane hit Florida, it became clear that the hurricane was going to wreak havoc in Louisiana and Mississippi. By this time, it was traveling at a speed of 175 miles per hour. The residents were told to evacuate, and over 80 percent of the population did. This was not a possibility for everyone, though. Some residents who could not evacuate stayed at home, and some went to the Superdome until the storm had passed.

The hurricane hit Louisiana, Mississippi, and Alabama. New Orleans, which is in Louisiana, was the worst affected area, and although the eye of the storm did not hit New Orleans on August 29th, another problem occurred due to the hurricane. The hurricane brought heavy rain, and fifty of the flood prevention levees surrounding the city failed, causing floods. The majority of the city was flooded. Those who stayed home had to climb on their roofs to stay safe.

An image of the flooding due to Hurricane Katrina
https://en.wikipedia.org/wiki/File:Hurricane_Katrina_Flooding.jpg

Although the Coast Guard rescued thirty-four thousand people in the city of New Orleans, the government did not seem to do enough to help the residents.[ix] People who had initially been in the Superdome and those who arrived after the storm were told vehicles were coming to help them evacuate. However, that didn't happen, and the majority didn't get evacuated.

When the flood subsided and the restoration process began, there was a grant for the residents who had lost their homes. However, it became difficult for many to receive their grants since they needed documentation of what had been lost in the hurricane. Black Americans faced discrimination, receiving less money than those who lived in white neighborhoods.[lxi]

The hurricane took almost two thousand lives. It resulted in people living in warzone-like conditions while waiting to be rescued and damaged homes. The hurricane devastated New Orleans to the point that rebuilding the area took over ten years. One positive result was that it caused the government to ensure that the levees would work better for future hurricanes. These improvements were seen when Hurricane Ida hit Louisiana, which caused less damage than Hurricane Katrina. Although Ida was smaller, it hit New Orleans more directly.

Financial Crisis of 2008

For those recovering from Hurricane Katrina, 2007 and the years that followed brought their own troubles. The year 2008 is known for the financial crisis that happened; however, it had started long before that.

In the 2000s, a housing bubble occurred. Housing prices went up, as did demand. Members of the public were buying houses at a higher rate than normal with the expectation of selling the house for more money than it was bought for. Banks in America also realized those profits could be capitalized upon and began to offer sub-prime mortgages. These were mortgages that were given to people who were normally denied the opportunity to get one. Sub-prime mortgages were given to people who had bad credit and people who had a low chance of being able to pay mortgages back. Similar to the Great Depression, the public and investors were thinking about what could be gained in the short term instead of what these transactions could do to the economy in the long term.[lxii] Furthermore, people didn't realize that their actions could have an effect on the global economy.

At the end of 2007, homeowners, many of whom had these sub-prime mortgages, were unable to pay their mortgages. This was the start of the financial crisis of 2008.

When it became apparent that there was an economic problem, banks did not want to loan each other money, which is a key component of the international banking system. Banks, such as Bear Stearns, began to fail. The Federal Reserve pumped money into Bear Steans in order to stop it from failing, and the investment bank was bailed out in March 2008.

But approximately six months later, the investment bank Lehman Brothers ran into problems and filed for bankruptcy. The Federal Reserve decided not to bail them out. The crisis was felt on Wall Street, which saw prices dip and continue to fall. September 2008 saw "the worst day on Wall Street since the Great Depression."[lxiii]

These events perpetuated the financial crisis in the US, and like the Great Depression, it affected the world. Banks like the Northern Rock in Britain ran into trouble as the United Kingdom's own housing bubble burst. The Irish banks began to fail in the autumn of 2008 as well, showing how global the crisis really was.

The financial crisis triggered mass unemployment in the US, and by October 2009, unemployment peaked at 10 percent.[lxiv]

The crisis made those in the finance world realize banks needed more regulations to prevent a similar event from occurring in the future. Since then, measures, such as stress testing, have been introduced, and banks have become more regulated to ensure a repeat would be hard to achieve.

Internationally and nationally, the 2000s in America were turbulent. It began with a presidential election that will continue to be talked about decades down the line. The devastating September 11th attacks saw a terrorist attack on US soil that affected the lives of

Americans forever. It led to the War on Terror, which resulted in a war in Afghanistan that ended up lasting for two decades. The War on Terror is blamed for the rise of extremist organizations, which have organized attacks in Europe and beyond long after 9/11. On a national basis, the financial crisis that hit America in this decade was a reminder of how connected each economy is around the world.

Conclusion

To say that American society changed greatly during the years between 1920 and 2010 would be an understatement.

World War Two shaped the world by forming two superpowers whose foreign policy was sometimes more aggressive than helpful when supporting nations around the world. Bringing the world to the possible brink of yet another global war was enough to stop the Soviet Union and the US from using their nuclear weapons.

The many wars of the 20th century led to destruction in different ways. The destruction left in Europe after World War Two and the atomic bombs used on Japan would have been enough destruction for a century or even two. Unfortunately, wars from Europe to Africa to the Middle East continued to rage as the superpowers fueled the conflicts to protect their nations and ideologies during the Cold War.

The Vietnam War was a pinnacle war in the lives of the Americans. It made the Americans reflect on their own opinion of war and how it affects their country and the country where it is being fought.

The 1960s helped to define the lines between the parties. American society took a more liberal approach, which resulted in the passing of the Voting Rights Act of 1965 and the Civil Rights Act the year before. Presidents like Lyndon B. Johnson passed legislation that helped the poor and elderly. On a political level, the lines were drawn. By the 1990s, it became clear that the political party divide was there, and many felt like they needed to pick a side: Democrat or Republican.

The story of recessions was often retold during this time too, spanning from the Great Depression to the stagflation that occurred in the 1970s to the recession that happened the decade after and the recession that began in 2007. This tells us that, although recessions are inevitable, regulation is necessary to ensure banks work for regular people instead of just for themselves. The recessions also teach us the danger of the population investing in the stock market and the housing market without the necessary education.

Two presidents, Richard Nixon and Bill Clinton, showed themselves to be human and were engulfed in scandals, namely the Watergate scandal and the Lewinsky scandal, respectively. The gift of journalism is what brought both of the presidents' actions to light, showing the importance of independent journalism.

One of the most exciting events that shaped the later 21st century was the fight for women's equality, with the world seeing fourth-wave feminism in action today. The influence music and literature had on society is a reflection of how necessary creativity is for a society to continue. Whether it be the Black American writers during the Harlem Renaissance, the feminist writers during the second wave of feminism, or the singers who protested the Vietnam War, creativity has had an important place in the lives of Americans.

The ability for companies to capitalize on the World Wide Web has taken many shapes and forms over the decades. Its explosion by the end of the 1990s showed that it was a necessary component of society and the global economy. It seems like it will certainly continue to be so.

Here's another book by Captivating History that you might like

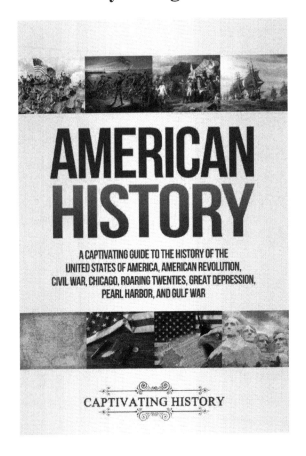

Free Bonus from Captivating History
(Available for a Limited time)

Hi History Lovers!

Now you have a chance to join our exclusive history list so you can get your first history ebook for free as well as discounts and a potential to get more history books for free! Simply visit the link below to join.

Captivatinghistory.com/ebook

Also, make sure to follow us on Facebook, Twitter and Youtube by searching for Captivating History.

Bibliography

ABC News. 17 Jun 2017. "Watergate: Inside the scandal that took down a presidency." [Video] Youtube.com.
https://www.youtube.com/watch?v=OZSGMMUC7FQ

"About Dr. Martin Luther King, Jr." https://thekingcenter.org/about-tkc/martin-luther-king-jr

Accessed: 1.4.2022

Allen, Frederick Lewis. *Since Yesterday: The 1930s in America, 3 September 1929–September 3, 1939.* Kindle Edition. New York. Open Road Media. 26 May 2015

Amadeo, Kimberly. 25 February 2022.
https://www.thebalance.com/president-jimmy-carter-s-economic-policies-4586571

"President Jimmy Carter's Economic Policies and Accomplishments." Accessed: 15.4.2022.

Andersen, Kurt. 6 February 2015. "The Best Decade Ever? The 1990s, Obviously."
https://www.nytimes.com/2015/02/08/opinion/sunday/the-best-decade-ever-the-1990s-obviously.html?_r=0 Accessed: 20.3.2022

Anderson, Joshua. *The Vietnam War: A Concise History of the Vietnam War from Beginning to End.* Kindle Edition. Independently published. 17 April 2017.

Appy, G, Christian. 26 March 2018. "What Was the Vietnam War About?" https://www.nytimes.com/2018/03/26/opinion/what-was-the-vietnam-war-about.html

Accessed: 14.3.2022

Apocalypse: The Second-World War. Directed by Clarke, Isabelle and Costelle, Daniel. Production Companies: CC&C Clarke Costelle & Cie, Établissement de Communication et de Production Audiovisuelle de la Défense (ECPAD), NHK. Release date: September 15, 2009. (France). Title of Site: Disney Plus.www.disneyplus.com

Bangel, Christian. Blickle, Paul. Erdmann, Elena. Faigle, Philip. Loos, Andreas. Stahnke, Julian. Tröger, Julius. Venohr, Sascha. 30 May 2019. "The Millions Who Left." https://www.zeit.de/politik/deutschland/2019-05/east-west-exodus-migration-east-germany-demography?utm_referrer=https%3A%2F%2Fwww.google.com%2F Accessed 19.4.2022

BBC News. 16 Oct 2016. "All That Jazz: How fashion helped liberate women in the 1920s." [Video] Youtube.com. https://www.youtube.com/watch?v=hpQ4mjxpXNA Accessed: 10.4.2022

Bennett Lowenthal. 25 October 1987. "The Jumpers of '29." https://www.washingtonpost.com/archive/opinions/1987/10/25/the-jumpers-of-29/17defff9-f725-43b7-831b-7924ac0a1363

Accessed: 3.5.2022

Berman, P. Elizabeth. 1 June 2019. "Trump is giving Arthur Laffer the Presidential Medal of Freedom. Economists aren't smiling."

https://www.washingtonpost.com/politics/2019/06/01/trump-is-giving-arthur-laffer-presidential-medal-freedom-economists-arent-laughing Accessed: 15.3.2022.

Biography.com "Editors." 27 April 2017. "Robert Kennedy." https://www.biography.com/political-figure/robert-kennedy. Accessed: 15.4.2022.

"Black History in Two Minutes or so." 31 Jan 2020. The Harlem Renaissance. [Video] Youtube.com. https://www.youtube.com/watch?v=9gboEyrj02g Accessed: 10.4.2022.

Brownsville Herald. [volume], October 28, 1929, Image 1.

https://chroniclingamerica.loc.gov/lccn/sn86063730/1929-10-28/ed-1/seq-1/#date1=1929&sort=date&date2=1929&words=&language=&sequence=1&lccn=&index=18&state=&rows=50&ortext=&proxtext=&year=&phrasetext=&andtext=&proxValue=&dateFilterType=yearRange&page=79 Accessed: 10.11.2021.

Brownsville Herald. [volume], October 30, 1929, Noon Edition, Image 1.

https://chroniclingamerica.loc.gov/lccn/sn86063730/1929-10-30/ed-2/seq-1/#date1=1929&sort=date&date2=1929&words=&language=&sequence=1&lccn=&index=40&state=&rows=50&ortext=&proxtext=&year=&phrasetext=&andtext=&proxValue=&dateFilterType=yearRange&page=79 Accessed: 10.11.2021.

Bourne, Stephen. *Under Fire.* Kindle Edition. Cheltenham, The History Press. 3 August 2020.

"Bush Out of These Troubled Times, a New World Order."

https://www.washingtonpost.com/archive/politics/1990/09/12/bush-out-of-these-troubled-times-a-new-world-order/b93b5cf1-e389-4e6a-84b0-85f71bf4c946 Accessed: 15.3.2022.

"Calvin Coolidge."

https://www.pbs.org/wgbh/americanexperience/features/presidents-coolidge

Accessed: 10.4.2022.

Charman, Terry. Professor Black, Jeremy. December 6, 2021. "WW2 timeline: 20 important dates and milestones you need to know." https://www.historyextra.com/period/second-world-war/timeline-important-dates-ww2-exact Accessed: 22.3.2022.

CNN. 7 Oct 2016. "What if the Cuban Missile Crisis led to war?" [Video] Youtube.com. https://www.youtube.com/watch?v=7XuV8J8jumE Accessed: 7.4.2022.

Cooley, Aaron. "War on Poverty." https://www.britannica.com/topic/War-on-Poverty

Accessed: 1.4.2022.

Crash Course. 21 Dec 2013. "Ford, Carter, and the Economic Malaise: Crash Course US History #42." [Video] Youtube.com. https://www.youtube.com/watch?v=pyN5LPHEQ_0

Accessed: 1.4.2022.

Crash Course. 6 December 2013. "The 1960s in America: Crash Course US History #40." [Video] Youtube.com. https://www.youtube.com/watch?v=lkXFb1sMa38

Accessed: 1.4.2022.

"Cuban Missile Crisis." https://www.bl.uk/learning/timeline/item108397.html

Accessed: 7.4.2022.

Curran, Enda. Golle, Vince. Scott, Malcolm. 10 March 2022. "World Economy Can Avoid 1970s Rerun, Albeit with Some Hurt." https://www.bloomberg.com/news/articles/2022-03-10/world-economy-can-avoid-1970s-rerun-but-not-without-some-hurt Accessed: 1.4.2022.

Davies, Nick. 22 April 2015. "Vietnam 40 years on: how a communist victory gave way to capitalist corruption." https://www.theguardian.com/news/2015/apr/22/vietnam-40-years-on-how-communist-victory-gave-way-to-capitalist-corruption Accessed. 29.3.2022.

December 8, 1941: Address to Congress Requesting a Declaration of War. [Transcript]. https://millercenter.org/the-presidency/presidential-speeches/december-8-1941-address-congress-requesting-declaration-war Accessed: 22.3.2022.

"Developments in crude oil prices." 3 April 2003.

https://treasury.gov.au/publication/economic-roundup-autumn-2003/developments-in-crude-oil-prices Accessed: 20.3.2022.

Dumenil, Lynn. *The Modern Temper. Farrar, Straus and Giroux.* Kindle Edition. New York City, Hill and Wang. 30 June 1995.

Educational Video Group. 13 October 2009. "Malcolm X Speech Democracy is Hypocrisy." [Video] Youtube.com. https://www.youtube.com/watch?v=qNfAFfu6VD0

Erin Blakemore. 23 March 2022. "What was the Cold War—and are we headed to another one?" https://www.nationalgeographic.com/culture/article/cold-war Accessed: 1.4.2022.

"Facts About Herbicides."

https://www.publichealth.va.gov/exposures/agentorange/basics.asp Accessed. 29.3.2022.

Ferrara, Peter. 30 Nov 2013. "The Great Depression Was Ended by the End of World War II, Not the Start of It." https://www.forbes.com/sites/peterferrara/2013/11/30/the-great-depression-was-ended-by-the-end-of-world-war-ii-not-the-start-of-it Accessed: 14 November 2021.

Fisher, Marc. 14 June 2012. "Watergate: The long shadow of a scandal."

https://www.washingtonpost.com/lifestyle/style/as-years-go-by-watergate-drifts-toward-myth/2014/06/14/cff4080c-aa8a-11e1-b15f-a61faf9b4d76_story.html

Folger, Jean. 18 March 2022. "What is stagflation? Understanding the economic phenomenon that stifled growth through the 1970s."

https://www.businessinsider.com/stagflation Accessed: 1.4.2022.

Fraser, Jeffery. 20 August 2019. "A Slow but Continuing Decline." *Pittsburgh Quarterly.* https://pittsburghquarterly.com/articles/a-slow-but-continuing-decline Accessed: 15.3.2022.

Friend, James. *World War Two: The United States of America at War.* Kindle Edition. 21 March 2015.

"Founding treaty." 03 May. 2022 (Last updated).

https://www.nato.int/cps/en/natolive/topics_67656.htm Accessed: 09.5.2022.

"General election campaign." https://www.britannica.com/event/United-States-presidential-election-of-1980/General-election-campaign Accessed: 15.3.2022.

"George H.W. Bush." https://www.pbs.org/wgbh/americanexperience/features/bush-george Accessed: 14.3.2022.

George W. Bush Presidency/September 22, 2001: Address on the U.S. Response to the Attacks of September 11. [Transcript]. https://millercenter.org/the-presidency/presidential-speeches/september-22-2001-address-us-response-attacks-september-11 Accessed: 11.4.2022.

Germany, Kent. "Lyndon B. Johnson: Domestic Affairs."

https://millercenter.org/president/lbjohnson/domestic-affairs Accessed: 1.4.2022.

Glass, Andrew. 04.15.2019. "US planes bomb Libya, April 15."

https://www.politico.com/story/2019/04/15/reagan-bomb-libya-april-15-1986-1272788 Accessed: 14.3.2022.

Goodier, Mandi. "The evolution of music: The music revolution of the 1960s." https://www.readersdigest.co.uk/culture/music/the-evolution-of-music-the-music-revolution-of-the-1960s Accessed: 1.4.2022.

"Great Depression and World War II, 1929-1945/Overview." https://www.loc.gov/classroom-materials/united-states-history-primary-source-timeline/great-depression-and-world-war-ii-1929-1945/overview Accessed: 16 April 2022.

Greatest Events of WWII in Colour. Directed by Boxer, Katie. Production companies: Head Gear Films, Metrol Technology, World Media Rights Productions. Release Date: November 8, 2019 (United Kingdom). Title of Site: Netflix. https://www.netflix.com/de-en

Greene, Robert, John. "Gerald Ford: Domestic Affairs."

https://millercenter.org/president/ford/domestic-affairs Accessed: 1.4.2022.

Greene, Robert, John. "Gerald Ford: Impact and Legacy."

https://millercenter.org/president/ford/impact-and-legacy Accessed: 1.4.2022.

Gregory, James. 2009.
https://depts.washington.edu/depress/hooverville.shtml Accessed: 9.5.2022

Greenberg, David. "Calvin Coolidge: Domestic Affairs."

https://millercenter.org/president/coolidge/domestic-affairs. Accessed: 10.4.2022.

Hart, Liddell, Basil. "North Africa campaigns."
https://www.britannica.com/event/North-Africa-campaigns Accessed: 20.3.2020.

Hastings, Sir Max. *Vietnam: An Epic History of a Divisive War 1945-1975.* Kindle Edition. London. HarperCollins Publishers. 20 September 2018.

Henderson, Jake. *Roaring Twenties: A Condensed History of America in the 1920s (History Brief Book 7)*. Kindle Edition. Reading Through History. 18 June 2016.

Herbert Hoover Presidency/March 4, 1929: Inaugural Address. [Transcript]. https://millercenter.org/the-presidency/presidential-speeches/march-4-1929-inaugural-address. Accessed: 10.11.2022.

Herbert Hoover Presidency/November 19, 1929: Statement on the Economy. [Transcript]. https://millercenter.org/the-presidency/presidential-speeches/november-19-1929-statement-economy. Accessed: 10.4.2022.

Hills, Rachel. 2 December 2014. "What Every Generation Gets Wrong About Sex." https://time.com/3611781/sexual-revolution-revisited/. Accessed: 1.4.2022.

History 101. Directed by: Tiley, Marc, Aroyo, Mira, Bower, Dick, Stevens, Laura. Production company: ITN Productions. Release date: May 22, 2020 (Brazil).

History Channel. 12 April 2018. "Here's How the Truman Doctrine Established the Cold War." [Video] Youtube.com. https://www.youtube.com/watch?v=Jb8aW46T3bg. Accessed: 9.5.2022.

History Channel. 29 Sept 2017. "The Formation of NATO and the Warsaw Pact." [Video] Youtube.com. https://www.youtube.com/watch?v=X1El1GVQVdc. Accessed: 09.5.2022.

History.com Editors. 2 Aug 2011. "Agent Orange." https://www.history.com/topics/vietnam-war/agent-orange-1. Accessed. 29.3.2022.

History.com Editors. 27 Oct 2009. "Bay of Pigs Invasion." https://www.history.com/topics/cold-war/bay-of-pigs-invasion#section_2.

Accessed: 7.4.2022.

History.com Editors. 27 October 2009. "Cold War History." https://www.history.com/topics/cold-war/cold-war-history. Accessed: 20.3.202.

History.com Editors. 24 November 2009. "Dr. Martin Luther King Jr. is assassinated." https://www.history.com/this-day-in-history/dr-king-is-assassinated. Accessed: 1.4.2022.

History.com Editors. October 27, 2009. "Dust Bowl." https://www.history.com/topics/great-depression/dust-bowl. Accessed: 9.5.2022.

History.com Editors 24 November 2009. "Former Yugoslav president Slobodan Milosevic goes on trial for war crimes." https://www.history.com/this-day-in-history/milosevic-goes-on-trial-for-war-crimes. Accessed: 15.3.2022.

History.com Editors. 17 Nov 2017. "Great Society."

https://www.history.com/topics/1960s/great-society. Accessed: 1.4.2022.

History.com Editors. 9 November 2009. "Hurricane Katrina." https://www.history.com/topics/natural-disasters-and-environment/hurricane-katrina. Accessed: 3.4.2022.

History.com Editors. 31 May 20117. "Just Say No."

https://www.history.com/topics/1980s/just-say-no. Accessed: 13.3.2022.

History.com Editors. 9 September 2019. "Marvin Gaye's hit single "What's Going On?" released." https://www.history.com/this-day-in-history/marvin-gaye-whats-going-on-released. Accessed: 1.4.2022.

History.com Editors. 13 November 2009. "Mao Zedong outlines the new Chinese government." https://www.history.com/this-day-in-history/mao-zedong-outlines-the-new-chinese-government. Accessed: 1.3.2022.

History.com Editors. 16 December 2009. "Oklahoma City Bombing." https://www.history.com/topics/1990s/oklahoma-city-bombing. Accessed: 20.3.2022.

History.com Editors. June 1, 2010. "Red Scare." https://www.history.com/topics/cold-war/red-scare. Accessed: 1.3.2022.

History.com Editors. "The Space Race." Feb 22, 2010.

https://www.history.com/topics/cold-war/space-raceAccessed: 1.4.2022.

History.com Editors. 29 October 2009. "Vietnam War."

https://www.history.com/topics/vietnam-war/vietnam-war-history. Accessed. 29.3.2022.

History.com Editors, Feb 22, 2010. "Vietnam War Protests."

https://www.history.com/topics/vietnam-war/vietnam-war-protests. Accessed:4.3.2022.

History.com Editors. February 9, 2010. "U.N. Charter signed."

https://www.history.com/this-day-in-history/u-n-charter-signed. Accessed: 20.4.2022.

History.com Editors, November 9, 2009. "World War II Potsdam Conference." (Updated 18 May 2021). https://www.history.com/topics/world-war-ii/potsdam-conference. Accessed: 20.3.2022.

History, Captivating. *American History: A Captivating Guide to the History of the United States of America, American Revolution, Civil War, Chicago, Roaring Twenties, Great Depression, Pearl Harbor, and Gulf War.* Kindle Edition. Captivating History. 8 February 2020.

History, Captivating. *History of Vietnam: A Captivating Guide to Vietnamese History.* Kindle Edition. Captivating History. 9 Dec. 2017.

History, Captivating. *The Space Race: A Captivating Guide to the Cold War Competition Between the United States and Soviet Union to Reach the Moon*. Kindle Edition. Captivating History. 28 September 2020.

History, Hourly. *Civil Rights Movement: A History from Beginning to End*. Kindle Edition. Hourly History. 2. August 2021.

History, Hourly. *Cold War: A History from Beginning to End (The Cold War)*. Kindle Edition. Hourly History. 20 Nov. 2016.

History, Hourly. *The Roaring Twenties: A History from Beginning to End*. Kindle Edition. Hourly History. 11 July 2017.

Housel, Morgan. *The Psychology of Money*. Kindle Edition. Hampshire. Harriman House. 8 September 2020.

"Housing 1929-1941." https://www.encyclopedia.com/education/news-and-education-magazines/housing-1929-1941. Accessed: 9.5.2022.

Hughes, Langston. "Let America Be America Again."

https://www.poetryfoundation.org/poems/147907/let-america-be-america-again. Accessed: 10.4.2022.

in60Learning. *Watergate: The Scandal That Changed US Politics Forever*. Kindle Edition.In60Learning. 21 Sept. 2019.

"Income Inequality." https://inequality.org/facts/income-inequality/. Accessed: 18.4.2022.

Jeremi Suri. *Power and Protest: Global Revolution and the Rise of Detente*. Kindle Edition. Cambridge Massachusetts, London. Harvard University Press. 1 April 2005.

Jimmy Carter Book: The Biography of Jimmy Carter. Kindle Edition. University Press. 31 Aug. 2021.

Jimmy Carter Presidency. October 24, 1978: Anti-Inflation Program Speech. [Transcript] https://millercenter.org/the-presidency/presidential-speeches/october-24-1978-anti-inflation-program-speech. Accessed: 15.4.2022.

"John F. Kennedy." https://www.whitehouse.gov/about-the-white-house/presidents/john-f-kennedy/. Accessed: 1.4.2022.

Jones, S. Martha. 7 August 2020. "For Black women, the 19th Amendment didn't end their fight to vote." https://www.nationalgeographic.com/history/article/black-women-continued-fighting-for-vote-after-19th-amendment. Accessed: 10.11.2021.

Jordan, A, Matthew. TED-Ed. 26 Sept 2016. "The history of the Cuban Missile Crisis." [Video]. Youtube.com. https://www.youtube.com/watch?v=bwWW3sbk4EU. Accessed: 7.4.2022.

Kagan, Neil. Hyslop, Stephen. 3 June 2019. "Top Secret maps reveal the massive Allied effort behind D-Day." https://www.nationalgeographic.com/history/history-magazine/article/invasion-of-normandy-d-day. Accessed: 20.3.2022.

Kiprop, Joseph. 8 August 2018. "Former Soviet Union (USSR) Countries." https://www.worldatlas.com/articles/what-countries-made-up-the-former-soviet-union-ussr.html. Accessed: 15.4.2022.

Klein, Christopher. 25 February 2019. "1929 Stock Market Crash: Did Panicked Investors Really Jump from Windows?" https://www.history.com/news/stock-market-crash-suicides-wall-street-1929-great-depression. Accessed: 3.5.2022.

Klein, Christopher. 28 February 2019. "Before FDR, Herbert Hoover Tried His Own 'New Deal.'" https://www.history.com/news/great-depression-herbert-hoover-new-deal. Accessed: 9.5.2022.

Las Vegas Age. [volume], October 26, 1929, Image 1. https://chroniclingamerica.loc.gov/lccn/sn86076141/1929-10-26/ed-1/seq-1/#date1=1929&sort=date&date2=1929&words=&language=&sequence=1&lccn=&index=1&state=&rows=50&ortext=&proxtext=&year=&phrasetext=&andtext=&proxValue=&dateFilterType=yearRange&page=79. Accessed: 10.11.2021.

Layton, Geoff. *Access to History: Democracy and Dictatorships in Germany 1919-63 for OCR Second Edition.* Kindle Edition. London. Hodder Education. 25 September 2015.

Little, Becky. 10 March 2022. "Soviet Union Leaders: Timeline." HISTORY. https://www.history.com/news/soviet-union-leaders-order. Accessed: 10.3.2022.

Longley, Robert. 8 May 2019. "The Reagan Doctrine: To Wipe Out Communism." https://www.thoughtco.com/the-reagan-doctrine-and-communism-4571021.

Accessed: 14.3.2022.

"Looking Back on the Warsaw Pact." https://learngerman.dw.com/en/looking-back-on-the-warsaw-pact/a-1582537. Accessed: 9.5.2022.

Luo, Feijun et al. "Impact of business cycles on US suicide rates, 1928-2007." American journal of public health vol. 101,6 (2011): 1139-46. doi:10.2105/AJPH.2010.300010. https://www.ncbi.nlm.nih.gov/pmc/articles/PMC3093269/. Accessed: 3.5.2022.

"Lyndon B. Johnson." https://www.pbs.org/wgbh/americanexperience/features/presidents-lyndon-b-johnson/. Accessed: 15.4.2022.

MACMILLAN, MARGARET. 11 September 2009. "Rebuilding the world after the second world war."

https://www.theguardian.com/world/2009/sep/11/second-world-war-rebuilding. Accessed: 22.3.2022.

"Major Cold War Events." https://www.britannica.com/study/major-cold-war-events. Accessed: 11.3.2022.

Mankiw, Gregory, N. 29 January 2016. To Grade Presidents on the Economy, Look at Policies, Not Results. https://www.nytimes.com/2016/01/31/upshot/to-grade-presidents-on-the-economy-look-at-policies-not-results.html. Accessed 14.4.2022.

Matthews, Dylan. 26 Nov 2016. "7 bizarre ways the US tried to kill or topple Fidel Castro - Vox." https://www.vox.com/2016/11/26/13752514/us-fidel-castro-assassination. Accessed: 14.3.2022.

McCurry, Justin. Mon 13 Dec 2021. "North and South Korea agree 'in principle' on formal end of war." https://www.theguardian.com/world/2021/dec/13/north-south-korea-agree-in-principle-formal-end-war-us. Accessed: 1.4.2022.

Merle, Renae, 10 September 2018. "A guide to the financial crisis — 10 years later." https://www.washingtonpost.com/business/economy/a-guide-to-the-financial-crisis--10-years-later/2018/09/10/114b76ba-af10-11e8-a20b-5f4f84429666_story.html. Accessed: 9.3.2022.

Moss, Charles. 9 February 2022. "Discover the history of Tennessee's forgotten music empire." https://www.nationalgeographic.com/travel/article/discover-the-history-of-tennessees-forgotten-music-empire. Accessed: 10.4.2022.

MSNBC. 15 Nov 2013. "Gov. Gavin Newsom Denies Parole for Robert F. Kennedy's Assassin." [Video] Youtube.com. https://www.youtube.com/watch?v=wYGYFY4Bq5c. Accessed: 15.4.2022.

Mudge, Rob. 08.02.2022. "What is NATO and why was it created?" https://www.dw.com/en/what-is-nato-and-why-was-it-created/a-60688639.

Accessed: 9.5.2022.

"Music in the Civil Rights Movement." https://www.loc.gov/collections/civil-rights-history-project/articles-and-essays/music-in-the-civil-rights-movement/. Accessed: 1.4.2022.

National Museum of American Diplomacy. "Tear Down This Wall." https://diplomacy.state.gov/tear-down-this-wall/. Accessed: 15.3.2022.

NBC News Learn. 30 Apr 2020. "The Dust Bowl and the Depression." [Video] Youtube.com.

https://www.youtube.com/watch?v=pJ9QOcVt1Hc. Accessed: 2.5.2022.

"Nixon archives released almost four decades after Watergate." 11 November 2011. https://www.bbc.com/news/av/world-15687918.

"Operation Jubilee: The Raid at Dieppe." 8 October 2021. https://www.nationalww2museum.org/war/articles/operation-jubilee-dieppe-raid-1942 Accessed: 20.3.2020.

President Clinton's 1996 State of the Union Address as delivered. https://clintonwhitehouse4.archives.gov/WH/New/other/sotu.html Accessed: 15.3.2022.

Press, A. 1 December 2018. "'Read my lips. No new taxes': quotes from President George HW Bush." https://www.theguardian.com/us-news/2018/dec/01/read-my-lips-no-new-taxes-quotes-from-president-george-hw-bush Accessed: 15.3.2022.

"Remembering the Battle of Berlin: The Soviet War Memorial at Tiergarten." 2 May 2020. https://www.nationalww2museum.org/war/articles/battle-of-berlin-memorial-tiergarten. Accessed: 20.3.2022.

"Revelations from the Russian Archives." https://www.loc.gov/exhibits/archives/sovi.html. Accessed: 7.4.2022.

"Richard M. Nixon." https://www.whitehouse.gov/about-the-white-house/presidents/richard-m-nixon/ Accessed. 29.3.2022.

"Robert F. Kennedy." https://www.jfklibrary.org/learn/about-jfk/the-kennedy-family/robert-f-kennedy. Accessed: 15.4.2022.

Roberts, Steven. V. 11 September 1988. "The Nation; Reagan's Social Issues: Gone but Not Forgotten." https://www.nytimes.com/1988/09/11/weekinreview/the-nation-reagan-s-social-issues-gone-but-not-forgotten.html. Accessed: 13.3.2022.

Sablik, Tim. 22 November 2013. "Recession of 1981–82." www.federalreservehistory.org Available at:

https://www.federalreservehistory.org/essays/recession-of-1981-82. Accessed: 13.3.2022.

Saunders, Jim. *Blind Spot: How Industry Rescued America's Great Depression Economy.* Kindle Edition. Grayhawk Press. 15 November 2020.

Schaller, Michael. (2010). *Ronald Reagan.* Oxford University Press, Incorporated, 10 Mar. 2011. pp.34–58.

Selverstone, J, Marc. "John F. Kennedy: Death of a President." https://millercenter.org/president/kennedy/death-of-the-president. Accessed: 1.4.2022.

Selverstone, J, Marc. "John F. Kennedy: Domestic Affairs."

https://millercenter.org/president/kennedy/domestic-affairs. Accessed: 1.4.2022.

"Sex, love and friendship." https://www.bl.uk/sisterhood/themes/sex-love-and-friendship. Accessed: 1.4.2022.

Shabad, Rebecca. 1 March 2022. https://www.nbcnews.com/politics/congress/house-passes-bill-make-lynching-federal-hate-crime-rcna18087.

Sharp, David. 4 September 2018). "3 decades on, George H.W. Bush's Points of Light still shine." https://apnews.com/article/075e1241829a4470ab96193e8d663c18. Accessed: 13.3.2022.

Shtrauchler, Nastassja. 13.11.2017. "How Nazis courted the Islamic world during WWII." https://www.dw.com/en/how-nazis-courted-the-islamic-world-during-wwii/a-41358387. Accessed: 22.3.2022.

Smithsonian Channel. 16 Feb 2018. "Malcolm X's Fiery Speech Addressing Police Brutality." [Video] Youtube.com. https://www.youtube.com/watch?v=6_uYWDyYNUg.

Stone, Roger J. *Tricky Dick: The Rise and Fall and Rise of Richard M. Nixon.* Kindle Edition. New York. Skyhorse. 11 July 2017.

"Soviet Union timeline." 31 October 2013.

https://www.bbc.com/news/world-europe-17858981. Accessed: 1.3.2022.

"The assassination of Dr. Martin Luther King Jr." https://millercenter.org/the-presidency/educational-resources/the-assassination-of-dr-martin-luther-king

Accessed: 1.4.2022.

"The Civil Rights Act of 1964." https://millercenter.org/the-presidency/educational-resources/the-civil-rights-act-of-1964. Accessed: 1.4.2022.

"The Dust Bowl." https://www.loc.gov/classroom-materials/united-states-history-primary-source-timeline/great-depression-and-world-war-ii-1929-1945/dust-bowl

Accessed: 2.5.2022.

The Editors of Encyclopedia. "Arab oil embargo." https://www.britannica.com/event/Arab-oil-embargo. Accessed: 1.4.2022.

The Editors of Encyclopedia Britannica. "Cairo Conference." https://www.britannica.com/event/Cairo-Conference. Accessed: 20.3.2022.

The Editors of Encyclopaedia Britannica. "Cotton Club." https://www.britannica.com/topic/Cotton-Club. Accessed: 10.4.2022.

The Editors of Encyclopedia Britannica. "Playboy." https://www.britannica.com/topic/Playboy#ref1261201. Accessed: 1.4.2022.

The Editors of Encyclopedia Britannica. "Tehran Conference." https://www.britannica.com/event/Tehran-Conference. Accessed: 20.3.2022.

The Editors of Encyclopaedia Britannica. "Tojo Hideki."

https://www.britannica.com/biography/Tojo-Hideki. Accessed: 20.3.2022.

The Editors of Encyclopaedia Britannica. "United States presidential election of 1968."

https://www.britannica.com/event/United-States-presidential-election-of-1968.

Accessed: 14.4.2022.

"The Fall of the Soviet Union." https://europe.unc.edu/iron-curtain/history/the-fall-of-the-soviet-union/. Accessed: 14.3.2022.

"The Great Depression." 22 NOVEMBER 2013.

https://www.federalreservehistory.org/essays/great-depression. Accessed: 16 April 2022.

"The Iran-Contra Affair."

https://www.pbs.org/wgbh/americanexperience/features/reagan-iran/. Accessed: 14.3.2022.

"The Jazz Age."

https://www.pbs.org/wgbh/americanexperience/features/monkeytrial-jazz-age/. Accessed: 10.4.2022.

"The Korean War."

https://www.pbs.org/wgbh/americanexperience/features/bomb-korean-war/ Accessed: 1.4.2022.

The Life Guide. 1 Nov 2019. "The Vietnam War Explained In 25 Minutes | Vietnam War Documentary." [Video] Youtube.com. https://www.youtube.com/watch?v=7tNTh6KlXXU. Accessed: 14.3.2022.

The New York Times. "Hurricane Katrina Aftermath: In the Shadow/Retro Report." [Video] Youtube.com. https://www.youtube.com/watch?v=hlLh9WoZxfk. Accessed: 3.4.2022.

The Pacifica Radio/UC Berkeley Social Activism Recording Project. "Anti-Vietnam War Protests."

https://guides.lib.berkeley.edu/c.php?g=819842&p=5850986. Accessed: 15.4.2022.

"The Pill and the Sexual Revolution."

https://www.pbs.org/wgbh/americanexperience/features/pill-and-sexual-revolution/. Accessed: 1.4.2022.

"The Truman Doctrine and the Marshall Plan."

https://history.state.gov/departmenthistory/short-history/truman/ Accessed: 9.5.2022.

The Washington Times (Washington [DC]), October 8, 1921, (FINAL HOME EDITION).
https://www.loc.gov/resource/sn84026749/1921-10-08/ed-1/?sp=1&r=0.59,0.585,0.346,0.129,0. Accessed: 10.11.2021.

The Washington Times (Washington [DC]), December 31, 1921, (FINAL HOME EDITION).
https://www.loc.gov/resource/sn84026749/1921-12-31/ed-1/?sp=1&r=0.149,0.156,0.925,0.344,0. Accessed: 10.11.2021.

The Weather Channel. 27 Aug 2016. "1930s Dust Bowl." [Video] Youtube.com. https://www.youtube.com/watch?v=-J_RbFkv82o. Accessed: 2.5.2022.

"Timeline of the Women's Liberation Movement."
https://www.bl.uk/sisterhood/timeline. Accessed: 1.4.2022.

"Timeline: The Dust Bowl."

https://www.pbs.org/wgbh/americanexperience/features/dust-bowl-surviving-dust-bowl/. Accessed: 2.5.2022.

Tyle, Chris. "Jazz History: The Standards (1920s)."

https://www.jazzstandards.com/history/history-2.htm. Accessed: 5.4.2022.

"United States real GDP growth rate 1930-2019."

https://www.statista.com/statistics/996758/rea-gdp-growth-united-states-1930-2019/. Accessed: 13.3.2022.

"United States Relations with Russia: The Cold War."
https://2001-2009.state.gov/r/pa/ho/pubs/fs/85895.htm. Accessed: 14.3.2022.

"United Nations vs NATO: The Differences."
https://humanitariancareers.com/united-nations-vs-nato-differences/. Accessed: 09.5.2022.

"VE Day: The fall of Nazi Berlin in pictures." 8 May 2020.
https://www.bbc.com/news/world-europe-52572544. Accessed: 20.3.2022.

Wall Street Journal. 6 Sept 2018. "Warren Buffett Explains the 2008 Financial Crisis." [Video] Youtube.com.
https://www.youtube.com/watch?v=k2VSSNECLTQ. Accessed: 9.3.2022.

Wall Street Journal. 25 Jun 2021. "What the Inflation of the 1970s Can Teach Us Today." [Video] Youtube.com.
https://www.youtube.com/watch?v=Am17uljm440. Accessed: 1.4.2022.

Westad, Odd Arne. *The Cold War: A World History.* Kindle Edition. London. Penguin. 31

August 2017.

"What is NATO?" https://www.nato.int/nato-welcome/index.html. Accessed: 09.5.2022.

"Whip Inflation Now (WIN)."

"Who was Martin Luther King, Jr.?" 15 January 2020
https://www.nationalgeographic.com/culture/article/martin-luther-king-jr. Accessed:
1.4.2022.

Winter Elizabeth. 16 December 2007. "Cotton Club of Harlem (1923)."

https://www.blackpast.org/african-american-history/cotton-club-harlem-1923/. Accessed:

10.4.2022.

"WW2 People's War."

https://www.bbc.co.uk/history/ww2peopleswar/timeline/factfiles/nonflash/a6651218.shtml. Accessed: 20.3.2022.

Woods, A. 19 May 2021. "Malcolm X's Most Iconic Speeches." [Video] Youtube.com. https://newsone.com/3903093/malcolm-x-most-iconic-speeches/.

"Your guide to the Watergate scandal that brought down President Richard Nixon." 14 April 2022. https://www.historyextra.com/period/20th-century/brief-guide-watergate-scandal-president-nixon-what-happened/. Accessed: 16.4.2022.

Endnotes

[i] Henderson, Jake. *Roaring Twenties: A Condensed History of America in the 1920s (History Brief Book 7)*. Kindle Edition. Reading Through History. 18 June 2016.

[ii] *The Washington Times (Washington [DC]), October 8, 1921, (FINAL HOME EDITION).* https://www.loc.gov/resource/sn84026749/1921-10-08/ed-1/?sp=1&r=0.59,0.585,0.346,0.129,0

[iii] Henderson, Jake. *Roaring Twenties: A Condensed History of America in the 1920s (History Brief Book 7)*. Kindle Edition. Reading Through History. 18 June 2016.

[iv] Hughes, Langston. "Let America Be America Again." https://www.poetryfoundation.org/poems/147907/let-america-be-america-again. Accessed: 10.4.2022.

[v] BBC News. 16 Oct 2016. "All That Jazz: How fashion helped liberate women in the 1920s." [Video] Youtube.com. https://www.youtube.com/watch?v=hpQ4mjxpXNA. Accessed: 10.4.2022.

[vi] Jones, S. Martha. 7 August 2020. "For Black women, the 19th Amendment didn't end their fight to vote." https://www.nationalgeographic.com/history/article/black-women-continued-fighting-for-vote-after-19th-amendment.

[vii] Shabad, Rebecca. 1 March 2022. https://www.nbcnews.com/politics/congress/house-passes-bill-make-lynching-federal-hate-crime-rcna18087.

[viii] Herbert Hoover Presidency/March 4, 1929: Inaugural Address. [Transcript]. https://millercenter.org/the-presidency/presidential-speeches/march-4-1929-inaugural-address. Accessed: 10.11.2022.

ix Brownsville herald. [volume], October 28, 1929, Image 1.

https://chroniclingamerica.loc.gov/lccn/sn86063730/1929-10-28/ed-1/seq-1/#date1=1929&sort=date&date2=1929&words=&language=&sequenc
e=1&lccn=&index=18&state=&rows=50&ortext=&proxtext=&year=&p
hrasetext=&andtext=&proxValue=&dateFilterType=yearRange&page=
79. Accessed: 10.11.2021.

x Allen, Frederick Lewis. *Since Yesterday: The 1930s in America, 3 September 1929–September 3, 1939.* Kindle Edition. New York. Open Road Media. 26 May 2015.

xi Henderson, Jake. *The Great Depression: A Condensed History of America in the 1930s (History Brief Book 8).* Kindle Edition. Reading Through History. 21 June 2016.

xii Saunders, Jim. *Blind Spot: How Industry Rescued America's Great Depression Economy.* Kindle Edition. Grayhawk Press. 15 November 2020.

xiii Ferrara, Peter. 30 Nov 2013. "The Great Depression Was Ended by the End of World War II, Not the Start of It."
https://www.forbes.com/sites/peterferrara/2013/11/30/the-great-depression-was-ended-by-the-end-of-world-war-ii-not-the-start-of-it/.
Accessed: 14 November 2021.

xiv Friend, James. *World War Two: The United States of America at War.* Kindle Edition. 21 March 2015.

xv *Greatest Events of WWII in Colour.* Directed by Boxer, Katie. Production companies: Head Gear Films, Metrol Technology, World Media Rights Productions. Release Date: November 8, 2019 (United Kingdom). Title of Site: Netflix. https://www.netflix.com/de-en/. Season 1, Episode, 3.

xvi December 8, 1941: Address to Congress Requesting a Declaration of War. [Transcript]. https://millercenter.org/the-presidency/presidential-speeches/december-8-1941-address-congress-requesting-declaration-war. Accessed: 22.3.2022.

xvii History, Captivating. *American History: A Captivating Guide to the History of the United States of America, American Revolution, Civil War, Chicago, Roaring Twenties, Great Depression, Pearl Harbor, and Gulf War.* Kindle Edition. Captivating History. 8 February 2020.

[xviii] Charman, Terry. Professor Black, Jeremy. December 6, 2021. "WW2 timeline: 20 important dates and milestones you need to know." https://www.historyextra.com/period/second-world-war/timeline-important-dates-ww2-exact/. Accessed: 22.3.2022.

[xix] Friend, James. *World War Two: The United States of America at War.* Kindle Edition. 21 March 2015.

[xx] *Greatest Events of WWII in Colour.* Directed by Uscinska, Kasia. Production companies: Head Gear Films, Metrol Technology, World Media Rights Productions. Release Date: November 8, 2019 (United Kingdom). Title of Site: Netflix. https://www.netflix.com/de-en/. Season 1, Episode 10.

[xxi] Bangel, Christian. Blickle, Paul. Erdmann, Elena. Faigle, Philip. Loos, Andreas. Stahnke, Julian. Tröger, Julius. Venohr, Sascha. 30. May 2019. "The Millions Who Left." https://www.zeit.de/politik/deutschland/2019-05/east-west-exodus-migration-east-germany-demography?utm_referrer=https%3A%2F%2Fwww.google.com%2F. Accessed 19.4.2022.

[xxii] Davies, Nick. 22 April 2015. "Vietnam 40 years on: how a communist victory gave way to capitalist corruption." https://www.theguardian.com/news/2015/apr/22/vietnam-40-years-on-how-communist-victory-gave-way-to-capitalist-corruption. Accessed. 29.3.2022.

[xxiii] History, Captivating. *History of Vietnam: A Captivating Guide to Vietnamese History.* Kindle Edition. Captivating History. 9 Dec. 2017.

[xxiv] Davies, Nick. 22 April 2015. "Vietnam 40 years on: how a communist victory gave way to capitalist corruption." https://www.theguardian.com/news/2015/apr/22/vietnam-40-years-on-how-communist-victory-gave-way-to-capitalist-corruption. Accessed. 29.3.2022.

[xxv] History, Hourly. *Civil Rights Movement: A History from Beginning to End.* Kindle Edition. Hourly History. 2. August 2021.

[xxvi] Hills, Rachel. 2 December 2014. "What Every Generation Gets Wrong About Sex." https://time.com/3611781/sexual-revolution-revisited/. Accessed: 1.4.2022.

[xxvii] "The Pill and the Sexual Revolution."

https://www.pbs.org/wgbh/americanexperience/features/pill-and-sexual-revolution/. Accessed: 1.4.2022.

[xxviii] History.com Editors. 24 November 2009. "Dr. Martin Luther King Jr. is assassinated." https://www.history.com/this-day-in-history/dr-king-is-assassinated. Accessed: 1.4.2022.

[xxix] Crash Course. 21 Dec 2013. "Ford, Carter, and the Economic Malaise: Crash Course US History #42." [Video] Youtube.com. https://www.youtube.com/watch?v=pyN5LPHEQ_0. Accessed: 1.4.2022.

[xxx] Jimmy Carter Presidency/ October 24, 1978: Anti-Inflation Program Speech. [Transcript] https://millercenter.org/the-presidency/presidential-speeches/october-24-1978-anti-inflation-program-speech. Accessed: 15.4.2022.

[xxxi] History.com Editors. "Senator Nixon Takes Tough Stand on Communism." https://www.history.com/topics/us-presidents/senator-nixon-takes-tough-stand-on-communism-video Accessed: 14.3.2022.

[xxxii] Glass, Andrew. 04.15.2019. "US planes bomb Libya, April 15." https://www.politico.com/story/2019/04/15/reagan-bomb-libya-april-15-1986-1272788 Accessed: 14.3.2022.

[xxxiii] "The Collapse of the Soviet Union." https://history.state.gov/milestones/1989-1992/collapse-soviet-union Accessed: 10.3.2022.

[xxxiv] "General election campaign." https://www.britannica.com/event/United-States-presidential-election-of-1980/General-election-campaign. Accessed: 15.3.2022.

[xxxvxxxv] Schaller, Michael. (2010). *Ronald Reagan.* Oxford University Press, Incorporated, 10 Mar. 2011. pp.34–58.

[xxxvi] History.com Editors. 31 May 20117. "Just Say No." https://www.history.com/topics/1980s/just-say-no. Accessed: 13.3.2022.

[xxxvii] Fraser, Jeffery. 20 August 2019. "A Slow but Continuing Decline." *Pittsburgh Quarterly.* https://pittsburghquarterly.com/articles/a-slow-but-continuing-decline/. Accessed: 15.3.2022.

xxxviii Roberts, Steven.V. 11 September 1988. "The Nation; Reagan's Social Issues: Gone but Not Forgotten." https://www.nytimes.com/1988/09/11/weekinreview/the-nation-reagan-s-social-issues-gone-but-not-forgotten.html. Accessed: 13.3.2022.

xxxix Sharp, David. 4 September 2018). "3 decades on, George H.W. Bush's Points of Light still shine." https://apnews.com/article/075e1241829a4470ab96193e8d663c18. Accessed: 13.3.2022.

xli Berman, P. Elizabeth. 1 June 2019. "Trump is giving Arthur Laffer the Presidential Medal of Freedom. Economists aren't smiling." https://www.washingtonpost.com/politics/2019/06/01/trump-is-giving-arthur-laffer-presidential-medal-freedom-economists-arent-laughing/. Accessed: 15.3.2022.

xlii Sablik, Tim. 22 November 2013. "Recession of 1981–82." www.federalreservehistory.org Available at: https://www.federalreservehistory.org/essays/recession-of-1981-82. Accessed: 13.3.2022.

xliii "United States real GDP growth rate 1930-2019." https://www.statista.com/statistics/996758/rea-gdp-growth-united-states-1930-2019/. Accessed: 13.3.2022.

xliv Kimberly Amadeo (2012). "US Debt by President: By Dollar and Percentage." https://www.thebalance.com/us-debt-by-president-by-dollar-and-percent-3306296. Accessed: 14.3.2022.

xlv Press, A. 1 December 2018. "'Read my lips. No new taxes': quotes from President George HW Bush." https://www.theguardian.com/us-news/2018/dec/01/read-my-lips-no-new-taxes-quotes-from-president-george-hw-bush Accessed: 15.3.2022.

xlvi President Clinton's 1996 State of the Union Address as delivered. https://clintonwhitehouse4.archives.gov/WH/New/other/sotu.html Accessed: 15.3.2022.

xlvi Longley, Robert. 8 May 2019. "The Reagan Doctrine: To Wipe Out Communism." https://www.thoughtco.com/the-reagan-doctrine-and-communism-4571021. Accessed: 14.3.2022.

xlviii "The Iran-Contra Affair." https://www.pbs.org/wgbh/americanexperience/features/reagan-iran/. Accessed: 14.3.2022.

xlix National Museum of American Diplomacy. "Tear Down This Wall." https://diplomacy.state.gov/tear-down-this-wall/. Accessed: 15.3.2022.

l "Bush Out of These Troubled Times, a New World Order." https://www.washingtonpost.com/archive/politics/1990/09/12/bush-out-of-these-troubled-times-a-new-world-order/b93b5cf1-e389-4e6a-84b0-85f71bf4c946/. Accessed: 15.3.2022.

li "George H.W. Bush." https://www.pbs.org/wgbh/americanexperience/features/bush-george/. Accessed: 14.3.2022.

lii History.com Editors 24 November 2009. "Former Yugoslav president Slobodan Milosevic goes on trial for war crimes." https://www.history.com/this-day-in-history/milosevic-goes-on-trial-for-war-crimes. Accessed: 15.3.2022.

liii "Developments in crude oil prices." 3 April 2003. https://treasury.gov.au/publication/economic-roundup-autumn-2003/developments-in-crude-oil-prices Accessed: 20.3.2022.

liv Andersen, Kurt. 6 February 2015. "The Best Decade Ever? The 1990s, Obviously." https://www.nytimes.com/2015/02/08/opinion/sunday/the-best-decade-ever-the-1990s-obviously.html?_r=0. Accessed: 20.3.2022.

lv Andersen, Kurt. 6 February 2015. "The Best Decade Ever? The 1990s, Obviously." https://www.nytimes.com/2015/02/08/opinion/sunday/the-best-decade-ever-the-1990s-obviously.html?_r=0. Accessed: 20.3.2022.

lvi "Income Inequality." https://inequality.org/facts/income-inequality/. Accessed: 18.4.2022.

lvii "Computer Ownership Up Sharply in the 1990s." https://www.bls.gov/opub/btn/archive/computer-ownership-up-sharply-in-the-1990s.pdf Accessed: 20.3.2022.

lviii History.com Editors. 16 December 2009. "Oklahoma City Bombing." https://www.history.com/topics/1990s/oklahoma-city-bombing. Accessed: 20.3.2022.

lix George W. Bush Presidency/September 22, 2001: Address on the U.S. Response to the Attacks of September 11. [Transcript]. https://millercenter.org/the-presidency/presidential-speeches/september-22-2001-address-us-response-attacks-september-11. Accessed: 11.4.2022.

[lx] History.com Editors. 9 November 2009. "Hurricane Katrina." https://www.history.com/topics/natural-disasters-and-environment/hurricane-katrina. Accessed: 3.4.2022.

[lxi] *The New York Times*. "Hurricane Katrina Aftermath: In the Shadow/Retro Report." [Video] Youtube.com. https://www.youtube.com/watch?v=hlLh9WoZxfk. Accessed: 3.4.2022.

[lxii] Morgan Housel. *The Psychology of Money*. Kindle Edition. Hampshire. Harriman House. 8 September 2020.

[lxiiilxiii] *Wall Street Journal*. 6 Sept 2018. "Warren Buffett Explains the 2008 Financial Crisis." [Video] Youtube.com. https://www.youtube.com/watch?v=k2VSSNECLTQ. Accessed: 9.3.2022.

[lxiv] Merle, Renae, 10 September 2018. "A guide to the financial crisis — 10 years later." https://www.washingtonpost.com/business/economy/a-guide-to-the-financial-crisis--10-years-later/2018/09/10/114b76ba-af10-11e8-a20b-5f4f84429666_story.html. Accessed: 9.3.2022.

Printed in Great Britain
by Amazon

18353253R00081